# Jagdgeschwader 53
# 'Pik As'

MAY 2008

OSPREY
PUBLISHING

# Jagdgeschwader 53 'Pik As'

John Weal
Series editor  Tony Holmes

**Front Cover**
Belying the travel brochures'
portrayal of the Mediterranean as
perennially warm and sunny, the
afternoon of 19 December 1941 over
the island of Malta was one of strong
winds, scudding clouds and driving
rain. Despite the appalling conditions
Major Günther *Freiherr* von
Maltzahn, who had arrived with
his *Geschwaderstab* JG 53 in Sicily
just four days earlier, took off from
Comiso to lead the four Bf 109F
fighters of his *Stabsschwarm* (HQ
Flight) on a *freie Jagd* sweep over
Malta in support of a raid on the
island by Ju 88 bombers.

It was almost by chance that von
Maltzahn's small force encountered
a larger group of RAF Hurricanes that
had been scrambled to intercept the
incoming bombers. The *Kommodore*
of the 'Ace of Spades' *Geschwader*
claimed one of the British machines
as his 50th kill of the war to date.
His victim was, in all likelihood,
Plt Off Edward 'Pete' Steele, one
of three Americans flying with No
126 Sqn, and the only RAF fighter
pilot reported lost over Malta on
19 December 1941.

The later Oberst von Maltzahn
would remain at the head of JG 53
until October 1943, by which time
his overall total had risen to 68 (the
last, a P-40F Warhawk, shot down
over Tunisia on 4 January 1943).
After serving as *Jafü Oberitalien*
(Fighter-leader Upper Italy) until
August 1944, he spent the remainder
of the war in staff positions and
died, aged just 42, in Düsseldorf
on 24 June 1953 (*Cover artwork
by Mark Postlethwaite*)

First published in Great Britain in 2007 by Osprey Publishing
Midland House, West Way, Botley, Oxford, OX2 0PH
443 Park Avenue South, New York, NY, 10016, USA
E-mail; info@ospreypublishing.com

ISBN 13: 978 1 84603 204 2

Edited by Tony Holmes
Page design by Mark Holt
Cover Artwork by Mark Postlethwaite
Aircraft Profiles by John Weal
Index by Alan Thatcher
Printed and bound in China through Bookbuilders

07 08 09 10 11    10 9 8 7 6 5 4 3 2 1

ACKNOWLEDGEMENTS
The author would like to thank the following individuals for their generous help
in providing information and photographs – Erich Brüning, Chris Goss,
Manfred Griehl, Uwe Hausen, Walter Matthiesen, Axel Paul, the late Michael
Payne, Dr Alfred Price, Jerry Scutts, Robert Simpson, Andrew Thomas and
Wolfgang Zittek

EDITOR'S NOTE
To make this best-selling series as authoritative as possible, the Editor would be
interested in hearing from any individual who may have relevant photographs,
documentation or first-hand experiences relating to the world's elite pilots, and
their aircraft, of the various theatres of war. Any material used will be credited to
its original source. Please write to Tony Holmes via e-mail at:
tony.holmes@osprey-jets.freeserve.co.uk

# CONTENTS

# EARLY DAYS

**V**ery few, if any, of the world's major air arms have made such abundant use of unit heraldry as did the German Luftwaffe of World War 2. The designs chosen – in the main by the units themselves – ran the whole gamut from the overtly political, through the geographical, the ornithological and the vaguely scatological, right down to the heavy-handedly comical.

Nearly a thousand such emblems have been recorded, although many remain unidentified to this day. But there is one example that is arguably far more familiar to the general public than any other. It has been supplied in decal form with numerous plastic model kits, it has been featured in countless comic books and it is an almost *de rigueur* decoration on any German 'fighter' (such as repainted T-6 Texans and the like) brought to the silver screen by Hollywood.

In effect, it has become a form of visual shorthand as the almost universally accepted symbol of the wartime Luftwaffe. It is, of course, the strikingly simple *'Pik-As'*, or 'Ace of Spades'.

But what of the unit that actually carried this famous device on its machines from the opening weeks of World War 2 until the final day of surrender?

The story begins on 15 March 1937. This was the date that saw the simultaneous activation of a *Stab* (HQ) and the first two *Gruppen* of a completely new *Jagdgeschwader*, JG 334, in the Rhine-Main area of western Germany.

The officer selected to command the unit was Oberst Bruno Loerzer, a long-time friend of Hermann Göring. The two had met early in World War 1 when Loerzer was training to be a pilot and Göring was serving in an infantry regiment. It was Loerzer who prompted Göring to transfer to the air arm. And it was Loerzer who piloted the future Reichsmarschall during the latter's first operational tour as a back-seat observer and photographer in the spring and early summer of 1915.

The two young leutnants made a formidable team. Each was awarded the Iron Cross, First Class, in the field for their combined efforts in obtaining vital reconnaissance photographs of French fortifications around Verdun. For three days they cruised low over the chain of enemy forts, Loerzer skidding the two-seat Albatros about the sky while Göring hung far out over the side and calmly and methodically shot away with his camera.

Both subsequently retrained as fighter pilots, and ended the war in

Good friends, and a highly successful reconnaissance crew in the early months of World War 1, it would appear that a quarter of a century later – towards the end of the Battle of Britain – relations between the then *General der Flieger* Bruno Loerzer, GOC II. *Fliegerkorps* (left), and his C-in-C, Reichsmarschall Hermann Göring, were no longer quite so cordial

**Oberst Loerzer's JG 334 was first equipped with the Arado Ar 68E. The overall pale grey machines displayed no kind of coloured trim as an aid to *Geschwader* identification. Some sources suggest that 1. *Staffel's* 'White 6', pictured here at Frankfurt-Rebstock, was the mount of future *Experte* Franz Götz**

command of *Jagdgeschwader* – Göring as *Kommandeur* of JG Nr I and Loerzer of JG Nr III. But after the German capitulation of November 1918 Loerzer had to make his living as a civilian. He opted for commerce and became a successful cigar salesman.

Flying was in his blood, however. And when, in March 1933 – just two months after Adolf Hitler and his Nazi party had come to power in Germany – his erstwhile crewmate, and now the new régime's Minister of Aviation, Hermann Göring, offered him the presidency of the *Deutsche Luftsportverband* (DLV), he jumped at the opportunity.

Divided into 16 regional groups, the DLV, as it was commonly abbreviated, was the umbrella organisation set up by the party to control all hitherto private and sports flying throughout the Reich. With the *Pour le mérite* at his throat, and with 41 wartime victories to his credit (he was the ninth-ranking German fighter pilot of World War 1), Bruno Loerzer was a charismatic figure whose leadership was to have a positive influence on DLV members both young and old alike.

He took these qualities with him when he joined the Luftwaffe proper, where he was tasked first with setting up I./JG 232 (the later I./ZG 2) at Bernburg on 1 April 1936, before subsequently being appointed *Geschwaderkommodore* of JG 334 the following year.

Loerzer's command was but one part of the Luftwaffe's ambitious expansion programme of spring 1937. His two component *Gruppen* had been brought into being in the manner that was customary during that period of rapid growth. Known as the 'mother-daughter' system, this entailed hiving off a cadre of experienced pilots and ground personnel from an existing *Gruppe*, or *Gruppen*, to provide a ready-made nucleus for a brand new unit.

Hauptmann Hubert Merhart von Bernegg's I./JG 334 had thus been formed around a core of personnel drawn from both I. and II./JG 134, while the 'mother' unit of Major Hans Detlev Herhudt von Rhoden's II./JG 334 had been that fountainhead of so much of the Luftwaffe's pre-war fighter strength – I./JG 132 'Richthofen' (see *Osprey Aviation Elite Units 1 - Jagdgeschwader 2 'Richthofen'* for further details). Both I. and II./JG 334 were composed initially of just two *Staffeln*, but each was to be brought up to full establishment by the activation of a third *Staffel* on 1 July 1937.

Equipped with Arado Ar 68E biplanes, the whole *Geschwader* first took up residence at Mannheim-Sandhofen. For Loerzer's *Stab* and I. *Gruppe*, this was a purely temporary measure, however. The Luftwaffe's rate of expansion was far outstripping the number of airfields available to accommodate it. New bases were being built as quickly as possible, but *Stab* and I./JG 334's assigned airfield – formerly a trotting racecourse on the southeastern outskirts of Wiesbaden – was still far from finished.

I./JG 334's arrival at Wiesbaden-Erbenheim in July 1937 was marked by a ceremonial parade through the town. To the strains of martial music provided by the band in the background, Oberleutnant Werner Mölders leads his 1. *Staffel* past the reviewing stand

Leaving II./JG 334 in sole possession of Mannheim, *Stab* and I. *Gruppe* were thus first obliged to spend several weeks at Frankfurt-Rebstock, before finally being able to occupy their newly completed base at Wiesbaden-Erbenheim in July 1937.

Situated some 40 miles apart on the eastern bank of the Middle Rhine, Mannheim and Wiesbaden would house the *Geschwader* right up until the outbreak of war and beyond. Charged with the aerial defence of this important central sector of the Franco-German border, the *Geschwader* led a remarkably sedentary existence in comparison to many of the other Luftwaffe *Jagdgruppen* of the time that were shuttled around like so many chess pieces during the final years of peace and the opening months of the new war in Europe.

There were, of course, *some* breaks in this home-based routine. The first of these occurred in the autumn of 1937, when the Arados of JG 334 participated in the large-scale manoeuvres held in northern Germany. There would also be gunnery camps for the pilots, with firing practice over the North Sea, as well as exercises for the groundcrews that were specifically designed to prepare them for any eventual war of movement.

Training did not always go strictly according to plan. A pair of I. *Gruppe* Arados has come to grief in a ploughed field on a hillside somewhere in northern Germany during the autumn manoeuvres of 1937

Early in 1938, the *Geschwader*'s Ar 68Es were replaced by the first models of Willy Messerschmitt's revolutionary new monoplane fighter, the Bf 109B. And in mid-March 1938 – just a few days after the *Anschluss*, or annexation of Austria into the Greater German Reich – JG 334 was ordered to fly its *Bertas*, via Bad Aibling, in Bavaria, to Wiener-Neustadt, where it was to stage a number of demonstration flights for the benefit of the local populace (see Osprey Aviation Elite Units 6 - *Jagdgeschwader 54 'Grünherz'* for further details). The *Geschwader*'s Bf 109s were soon back guarding the Rhine, however.

In addition to its various manoeuvres, exercises and demonstrations, the Luftwaffe was also currently involved in a more covert undertaking. Pilots were quietly being posted away from their units for lengthy periods of time. One such individual was a certain Werner Mölders, who had been among the cadre supplied by II./JG 134 to help form I./JG 334, and who had been serving as *Kapitän* of the latter's 1. *Staffel* since its inception.

On 13 April 1938 Oberleutnant Werner Mölders took leave of 1./JG 334, his destination, Spain. There, he succeeded Adolf Galland as *Kapitän* of 3.J/88, the third *Staffel* of the *Legion Condor*'s fighter arm. Mölders was just one of a number of future Luftwaffe *Experten* who underwent their baptism of fire during the Spanish Civil War. But when he returned to Germany at the end of 1938 with 14 Republican aircraft to his credit, Mölders had proved himself the most successful of them all. He had also rewritten the rule book on fighter combat.

In fact, Mölders was to spend several weeks at the RLM (Air Ministry) in Berlin putting his experiences down on paper and drafting a new handbook on fighter tactics. His most important innovation was the scrapping of the outmoded 'vic' of three aircraft flying in arrowhead formation – a leader and two wingmen – and replacing them with a formation of four, consisting of two mutually supporting pairs. It is perhaps worth recording that not only did the RAF and the USAAF subsequently adopt this practice after the outbreak of war, it remains the standard basic fighter formation to this day.

By the time the now Hauptmann Werner Mölders returned to Wiesbaden-Erbenheim in mid-March 1939 to resume command of his 1. *Staffel* a lot had happened.

Oberst Bruno Loerzer had already left the *Geschwader* for the first of a succession of staff appointments a fortnight prior to Mölders' departure for Spain. His place at the head of JG 334 had been taken by Oberstleutnant Werner Junck on 1 April 1938. In the weeks that followed, the first Bf 109Ds began to arrive. And on 1 July 1938 moves were made to bring the *Geschwader* up to full establishment strength by the addition of a third *Gruppe*.

**Transition from the Arados to Willy Messerschmitt's new Bf 109 monoplane fighter could be even more dangerous. According to a *Gruppe* member, this photograph depicts the scene of the memorial service held at Wiesbaden-Erbenheim for 3. *Staffel*'s Obergefreiter Kreidt, killed in a flying accident on 3 June 1938**

Initially, III./JG 334 consisted of just one *Staffel*. It was not until 1 August that a *Gruppenstab* and the remaining two *Staffeln* actually came into being. Command of the *Gruppe* was given to Hauptmann Walter Schmidt-Coste, previously the *Kapitän* of 4./JG 334. The first *Staffel* had been equipped with Ar 68Es, but the whole *Gruppe* was to begin converting onto Bf 109Ds before August was out.

The Luftwaffe may have been supplying its units with the latest types of aircraft, but the thorny problem of housing them all remained unresolved. The airfield construction programme was still lagging a long way behind the output of machines and the creation of new units. It had originally been intended to base III./JG 334 at Mainz-Finthen, but this site was so far behind schedule that Schmidt-Coste's *Gruppe* had to share Mannheim-Sandhofen with II./JG 334.

Meanwhile, other elements of the *Geschwader* had again been attending summer gunnery camp on the island of Wangerooge, in the North Sea. References then differ as to the activities of JG 334 during the tense days of the Munich crisis in late September 1938. Most sources suggest that Oberstleutnant Junck's three *Gruppen* were retained at Wiesbaden and Mannheim on homeland defence duties. This would seem to make sense, as there was a very real fear in Germany at the time that France might react strongly in the face of Hitler's pressing demands for the Sudeten territories of Czechoslovakia to be ceded to the Reich. One reference work, however, maintains that a solitary *Gruppe* followed the route taken during the annexation of Austria in the spring by staging via Bad Aibling to Wiener-Neustadt, where it was held at readiness for the duration of the crisis.

Delayed by the intervening Austrian and Sudeten actions, the reorganisation of the Luftwaffe's command structure back in April – in which the six existing *Luftkreiskommandos* had been replaced by three main *Luftwaffengruppenkommandos* – finally resulted in the re-numbering of all fighter units on 1 November 1938. But for JG 334, the changes on this date went far beyond simple redesignation.

Firstly, the short-lived III. *Gruppe* was detached from the *Geschwader* altogether. Transferred to Gablingen, near Augsburg, it there joined the ranks of the so-called 'heavy' fighter arm as I./ZG 144 (later to become the famous II./ZG 76 'Sharksmouth' *Zerstörergruppe*).

More mystifying, perhaps, was the disbandment of Oberstleutnant Junck's *Geschwaderstab* on this same 1 November. In its place he inherited the so-called 'Stab Regensburg'. Quite where this staff had come from (apart from Regensburg, of course!), and what its previous duties had been, is unclear. But it was this unit that now assumed the mantle of *Stab JG 133* in line with the new High Command directive, while Junck's two remaining component *Gruppen* were likewise redesignated to become I. and II./JG 133.

During the winter of 1938/39, the *Geschwader* began to take delivery of its first Bf 109Es. And on 1 February 1939 another round of command restructuring – this time into *Luftflotten* – led to the emergence two months later of Junck's *Geschwader*, still only two-*Gruppen* strong, as JG 53. It was the third *Jagdgeschwader* (after JGs 51 and 52) commanded by *Luftflotte* 3 in the southwestern quadrant of Adolf Hitler's Greater German Reich.

# SITZKRIEG AND BLITZKRIEG

hen Germany invaded Poland in the early hours of 1 September 1939, Oberstleutnant Werner Junck's two *Gruppen* were still firmly ensconced at Wiesbaden and Mannheim, just as they had been (purportedly) a year earlier during the Sudeten crisis. Hitler was again concerned about the French reaction to his latest seizure of territory, and this time he had every reason to be. Poland was not going to fall into his lap as the result of yet another bloodless coup, as it was being invaded by overwhelming force of arms. It was a step too far by the *Führer*, and one that the western allies could not ignore. On 3 September Britain and France declared war on Germany.

Suddenly, the pilots of JG 53 found themselves in the frontline. And not just in the frontline, but in the most strategically important sector of the only common land border between Germany and France. The *Geschwader*'s area of operations stretched from Saarbrücken up to Trier. This took in the *Dreiländereck* – or three-nations corner – the point at which the frontiers of Luxembourg, France and Germany all met. Beyond this, Germany's western border abutted those of neutral Luxembourg, Belgium and Holland all the way up to the North Sea.

**Although still based at Wiesbaden-Erbenheim upon the outbreak of war, elements of I./JG 53 were dispersed to a meadow outside the base as a precautionary measure against possible enemy air attack**

The *Geschwader* had long been preparing for the eventuality of hostilities in the west. This photograph, taken in early 1939 (note the anonymous II. *Gruppe Dora* in the background) could be any group of Luftwaffe fighter pilots. But the maps they are studying clearly show the distinctive outline of the *Dreiländereck*, the area over which JG 53 would operate throughout the 'Phoney war'

During the early months of the war, the neutrality of these countries was strictly observed, and aircraft of the warring powers were forbidden to overfly their airspace. So, although no heavy bombing raids followed hard on the heels of France's declaration of war, JG 53's two *Gruppen* soon found themselves in the thick of things as the *Dreiländereck* 'junction' quickly became the main point of entry for French, and French-based RAF, reconnaissance aircraft sent into Germany. The Allied machines would first have to negotiate this southern tip of Luxembourg before heading northwards, *behind* the Belgian and Dutch borders, to photograph such areas as the industrial heartland of the Ruhr and its surrounding defences.

But the *Geschwader*'s first two victories of the war were to be claimed close to Saarbrücken along the southern, quieter end of its patrol sector. It was shortly before midday on 9 September that a pair of Bf 109Es of 1./JG 53 spotted a lone Bloch MB 131 reconnaissance-bomber of the *Armée de l'Air* high to the northeast of Saarbrücken. The enemy machine immediately turned away to starboard, diving hard for the safety of the border. The two Messerschmitts rapidly overhauled it, and the leading fighter, flown by Oberfeldwebel Walter Grimmling, opened fire at short range and set the Bloch's starboard engine on fire. Trailing a thin streamer of smoke, the bomber crossed the border, still in a steep dive.

Ordered not to enter French airspace, the two *Emils* were forced to break off the chase and Grimmling lost sight of his victim, which he had identified – incorrectly – as a British Blenheim. Confirmation that it had crashed was subsequently received from German ground troops in the area.

Some three hours later, 3./JG 53's Leutnant Wilhelm Hoffmann also claimed a kill – this time an obsolescent Bloch MB 200 bomber – in the same region.

The unit's first Iron Crosses. 1./JG 53's Oberfeldwebel Walter Grimmling (left) claimed the *Geschwader*'s first victory of the war – a 'Blenheim' downed near Saarbrücken on 9 September 1939. Unteroffizier Heinrich Bezner (right) was credited with one of the three Mureaux 115s shot down in the same area the following day

Oberfeldwebel Grimmling's *Staffelkapitän*, Hauptmann Werner Mölders, had not been aloft on that 9 September. Twenty-four hours earlier he had suffered engine damage during an otherwise inconclusive encounter with half-a-dozen French Hawk H-75A fighters. He attempted to nurse his *Emil* back to base at Wiesbaden, but was less than halfway there when the engine threatened to quit altogether and he had to make a forced landing in an open meadow near Birkenfeld. The machine somersaulted and Mölders sustained a painful – albeit not serious – back injury. His condition was, however, bad enough to keep him out of action for the next 11 days, during which time I./JG 53 increased its overall total of kills to six – including a second for Walter Grimmling – and suffered its first fatality (3. *Staffel*'s Unteroffizier Dill was lost in unknown circumstances on 19 September).

It was on 20 September that Werner Mölders scored his first victory of World War 2 – one of a trio of French H-75As bounced by 1. *Staffel* between Contz and Sierck, at the very apex of the *Dreiländereck*. Mölders' own combat report gives the bare facts;

'I took off with my *Schwarm* (section of four aircraft) at 1427 hrs to intercept six enemy monoplanes reported south of Trier. As the *Schwarm* overflew the River Saar near Merzig at 4500 metres, six machines were sighted south of Conz (*sic*) at 5000 metres. I climbed above the enemy in a wide curve to the north and carried out a surprise attack on the rearmost machine. I opened fire from approximately 50 metres, whereupon the Curtiss began to fishtail. After a further lengthy burst, smoke came out of the machine and individual pieces flew off it. It then tipped forward into a dive and I lost sight of it, as I had to defend myself against other opponents newly arriving on the scene.'

Mölders' success was confirmed by his three *Schwarm* members, who further reported that the French pilot bailed out before the Hawk crashed in flames to the west of Merzig.

The twentieth of September was also the day the Mannheim-based II./JG 53 opened its scoresheet. The first entry went to Oberleutnant Heinz Bretnütz, the *Kapitän* of 6. *Staffel*, who downed a French observation balloon at 0955 hrs (2./JG 53's *Stabsfeldwebel* Ignaz Prestele had destroyed a balloon two hours earlier, this being the first of three lost by the French in the area south of Saarbrücken on this date). But the true identity of the *Gruppe*'s second and third kills of 20 September – a pair of 'Blenheims' claimed by pilots of 5./JG 53 within a minute of each other over Bitche, on the French side of the border – remains a mystery.

As the first month of the war neared its end, I. and II./JG 53 continued to bring down the occasional enemy aircraft and balloon – four confirmed for I. *Gruppe* (including another balloon for 'Igel' Prestele), and six for II. *Gruppe*. Against this, II./JG 53 had to record its first casualty when 6. *Staffel*'s Feldwebel Hellge was reportedly lost in action against French Morane-Saulnier fighters over Bergzabern on 22 September.

Then, on 30 September, a sudden flurry of activity not only resulted in the heaviest air action over the western front to date, but also brought JG 53 its first confirmed RAF kills of the war.

The day began, however, with the destruction of a solitary French Potez 63 reconnaissance aircraft by Hauptmann Günther *Freiherr* von Maltzahn, *Kommandeur* of II. *Gruppe*, over the Saarbrücken area in the

Pictured in front of the DFS (German Gliding Research Institute) hangar at Darmstadt-Griesheim are the five pilots of 2./JG 53 who destroyed an entire formation of RAF Fairey Battles west of Saarbrücken on 30 September 1939. They are, from left to right, Unteroffizier Josef 'Sepp' Wurmheller, Unteroffizier Franz Kaiser, Oberleutnant Rolf Pingel (*Staffelkapitän*), Stabsfeldwebel Ignaz 'Igel' Prestele and Unteroffizier Hans Kornatz

late morning. This was the first victory credited to future Oak Leaves *Experte* and *Geschwaderkommodore* 'Henri' Maltzahn.

Shortly after the demise of the Potez, which crash-landed in flames in France, a formation of five Fairey Battles of the RAF's No 150 Sqn approached the same Saarbrücken-Merzig sector on a high-altitude photographic reconnaissance mission. The British machines were intercepted by eight *Emils* of 2./JG 53 and all of them were destroyed.

The first fell to the guns of *Staffelkapitän* Oberleutnant Rolf Pingel close to the target area. The last was chased some 32 kilometres back into French territory by Unteroffizier Josef Wurmheller, who riddled it with cannon and machine gun fire before breaking off the pursuit. 'Sepp' Wurmheller confidently claimed the Battle destroyed, as indeed it was. Although the pilot managed to get the crippled machine back to No 150 Sqn's base near Chalons, it burst into flames the moment it came to rest and was a complete write-off.

In the course of two further engagements later that same afternoon, pilots of 3. and 5. *Staffeln* were credited with another seven French aircraft, making the *Geschwader*'s total for the day 13!

These air actions of late September 1939 were carried out against a backdrop of equally hectic activity on the ground at Wiesbaden and

Other elements of the *Geschwader* did not fare so well against French Hawk H-75A fighters on that same 30 September. Four pilots were killed and a fifth belly-landed his damaged 'White 10' (of 1. *Staffel*) near Wiesbaden

Officers of the newly activated
III./JG 53 at Wiesbaden-Erbenheim in
the autumn of 1939. They are, from
left right, Leutnant Friedrich-Karl
Müller, an unidentified oberleutnant
of ground personnel (dark collar
tabs), Hauptmann Werner Mölders
(*Gruppenkommandeur*) and
Oberleutnant Hans von Hahn
(*StaKa* 8./JG 53)

Mannheim. The reason for this was that the *Geschwader* was again in the process of being raised to full three-*Gruppe* status, but this time there was no obliging 'mother' unit to provide the necessary nucleus. The *Geschwader* was left very much to its own devices, and elements of both I. and II. *Gruppen* were utilised to form the new III./JG 53.

The unit was officially activated during the last week of September at Wiesbaden-Erbenheim, I./JG 53 having been transferred forward to Kirchberg, in the Hunsrück – the high ridge of ground between the Rhine and Moselle valleys – to make room for the new *Gruppe*. Command of III./JG 53 was entrusted to Hauptmann Werner Mölders, who wasted little time in declaring the unit operational on 10 October 1939.

It was also during this period that the famous 'Ace of Spades' badge came into being, introduced at the suggestion of Generalmajor *Dipl.Ing.* Hans Klein, who had succeeded Oberstleutnant Werner Junck as *Kommodore* of JG 53 on 1 October. According to his own account, Klein first asked members of the *Geschwader* whether there should be a series of individual *Gruppe* and *Staffel* badges, or one emblem for the whole unit. The latter was decided upon, as it was felt that this would promote a stronger scnsc of '*Geschwader* loyalty and comradeship'. And so the iconic 'Ace of Spades' motif was chosen, and stencilled on both sides of the engine cowlings of all the Messerschmitts assigned to JG 53. It would still be in evidence when Germany surrendered in the spring of 1945.

By mid-October 1939, the opposing ground armies had reached that point of stalemate that would earn the first eight months of hostilities on the western front the nickname of the 'Phoney war' or *Sitzkrieg*. In the air

In October 1939 *Geschwaderkommodore* Generalmajor Hans Klein – pictured here (right) with Werner Mölders – was responsible for introducing the famed 'Ace of Spades' badge . . .

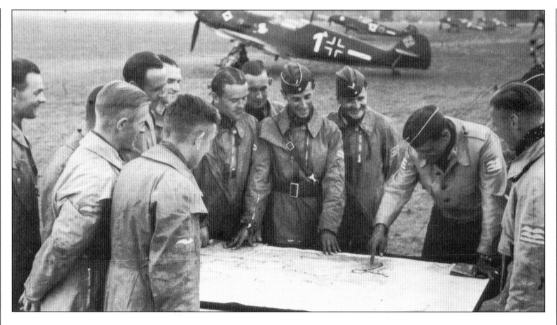

. . . which can just be made out on the *Emils* in the background of this shot of another II. *Gruppe* map session. The oberleutnant doing the pointing is Hubert Kroeck, the *Kapitän* of 4. *Staffel*, and that is his 'White 1' behind him. Note that, in addition to the new unit badge on the cowling, the machine also sports Kroeck's personal 'white top hat' motif below the windscreen

too, as the autumn weather began to give way to the winter of 1939/40 – one of the harshest in the region in living memory – activity was winding down, and at times coming to a complete standstill.

At Kirchberg, where the grassy surface soon became waterlogged with the constant autumn rains, Hauptmann Lothar von Janson's I./JG 53 found conditions particularly difficult. Ox-drawn carts had to be used to take fuel out to the dispersed aircraft. The *Gruppe* did not claim a single victory throughout the whole of October.

II./JG 53 at Mannheim-Sandhofen was more fortunate, but even its total tally for the month was just two Blenheims. The first of these, a No 57 Sqn machine piloted by Wg Cdr H M A 'Wings' Day, had taken off from its base in France to reconnoitre the northern reaches of the Ruhr. That 13 October was one of the rare fine days between the otherwise long periods of rain. There was not a cloud in the sky as the Blenheim successfully negotiated the *Dreiländereck*. Hardly had it begun to swing

Another example of the many personal emblems carried by 4./JG 53's fighters during the opening weeks of the 'Phoney war' was the 'laughing cow' that adorned Unteroffizier Erwin Weiss' 'White 4'. Weiss would be the first pilot of JG 53 to fall victim to the RAF when he was shot down by a Hurricane of No 73 Sqn on 7 April 1940

northwards, however, when it was intercepted near Birkenfeld by a pair of Bf 109Es of 4./JG 53 and promptly shot down in flames by Oberfeldwebel Ernst Vollmer.

Another brief break in the weather on 30 October enabled 5. *Staffel*'s Unteroffizier Joachim Hinkeldey to also to claim a Blenheim – this time east of Trier – although the actual identity of his victim cannot be established.

Significantly, perhaps, it was on this date, and in the very same area, that Werner Mölders opened the scoreboard for his new III./JG 53 with the destruction of a Blenheim. He was at the head of the *Gruppenschwarm*, leading a dozen *Emils* of 9. *Staffel* on patrol against enemy reconnaissance aircraft reported in the Bitburg-Merzig area, when;

'I noticed flak activity near Trier. I closed up to within 50 metres of the enemy machine undetected and could quite clearly see the British roundels. I opened fire from the shortest range possible. There was no return fire from the rear gunner, and the left engine emitted a thick cloud of white smoke, which quickly changed to black. As I pulled up alongside it, the aircraft was completely on fire. I observed a parachute, but it appeared to be smouldering. The Blenheim crashed near Klüsserath on the River Moselle.'

This Blenheim – a machine of No 18 Sqn, which came down some nine miles east-northeast of Trier – was the only RAF bomber to be lost on the central sector of the western front on this date.

With the *Gruppenkommandeur* having broken their duck, the pilots of III./JG 53 went on to claim seven of the *Geschwader*'s eleven November successes. Among these seven was a quartet of French Potez reconnaissance aircraft brought down west of Saarbrücken on 7 November, one of which provided a first for future Swords recipient Oberleutnant Wolf-Dietrich Wilcke, *Kapitän* of 7. *Staffel*.

Members of the RAD (Reich Labour Service) prepare to clear the wreckage of what is reported to be Werner Mölders' second kill – a Blenheim of No 18 Sqn RAF that he brought down over the Moselle on 30 October 1939. The numerals faintly visible on the undersurface of the wing bear no apparent relationship to the serial number of Mölders' victim on that date, however

9. *Staffel* groundcrew manhandle 'Yellow 7' across a decidedly damp apron at Wiesbaden in late 1939. Note the striking segmented camouflage scheme that III. *Gruppe* has introduced to replace the regulation dark green finish of their *Emils* as initially delivered – also the oversized, full chord-width uppersurface wing crosses (extended across the flaps) and the Arado Ar 68E parked in the background

This photograph was also taken towards the end of 1939 at Wiesbaden, and it shows Hauptmann Mölders (foreground right, facing camera) regaling air- and groundcrew of his *Gruppenstab* with details of his latest encounter with the enemy – possibly that which resulted in his third victory (a No 73 Sqn Hurricane) claimed over French territory on 22 December

December's only two victories were the result of the first ever engagement between German and British fighters in World War 2. It was the 22nd of the month, and elements of III./JG 53 were providing top cover for a pair of Dornier Do 17 reconnaissance machines some 12 miles inside French airspace when they spotted three enemy fighters far below. Werner Mölders was again in the lead as the *Emils* dived on the apparently unsuspecting trio. He put an accurate burst of fire into the aircraft on the left – initially identifying it as a French Morane-Saulnier – which went down in flames to crash close to a village.

Shortly afterwards Oberleutnant Hans von Hahn, the *Kapitän* of 8. *Staffel*, sent a second machine spinning and tumbling into a nearby forest, where it too burst into flames on impact. The two fighters, both of which had gone down about ten miles northeast of Metz, were not Morane-Saulnier MS.406s, however, but Hurricanes of the RAF's No 73 Sqn.

Apart from this one action, there was little aerial activity in December. But the month did see several changes on the ground. I./JG 53 was finally relieved of its unequal struggle against Kirchberg's mud and slush and was transferred down to Darmstadt-Griesheim, roughly equidistant between Wiesbaden and Mannheim.

On 19 December the *Geschwader*, which until this time had been subordinated directly to *Luftgaukommando* XII in a nominally purely defensive role, was placed under the command of *Luftflotte* 3 – one of the two air fleets gathering strength along Germany's western borders in preparation for the planned invasion of France early in the new year.

And on 21 December Generalmajor *Dipl.Ing.* Hans Klein relinquished his short-held command of the *Geschwader* upon being appointed to the office of *Jafü* 3 (Leader of Air Fleet 3's fighter forces). The officer selected to replace him as *Kommodore* of JG 53 was Major Hans-Jürgen von Cramon-Taubadel, ex-*Gruppenkommandeur* of I./JG 54, who would take over on 1 January 1940.

With winter refusing to release its icy grip, the first two months of 1940 were almost entirely uneventful. The only success during this lean period was a single MS.406 brought down south of Perl, close to the *Dreiländereck*, by Leutnant Walter Radlick of the *Gruppenstab* III./JG 53 on 10 January.

But in March 1940 activity in the air finally began to pick up again. The indefatigable III. *Gruppe* – its individual *Staffeln* now operating on a rotational basis out of Trier-Euren, hard by the Luxembourg border – took a limited, but steady, toll of French and British machines throughout the month. By month-end, the *Gruppe* had added nine more victories to its collective total, with *Kommandeur* Hauptmann Werner Mölders having doubled his existing score to six in the process.

By contrast, II./JG 53 crammed all its March successes into one frenetic ten-minute engagement on the last day of the month.

It was mid-afternoon when 20 *Emils* of Hauptmann von Maltzahn's *Gruppe* chanced upon a somewhat disorganised formation of MS.406s southwest of Saargemünd. Choosing their moment, the Messerschmitts pounced, claiming six of the eleven French fighters destroyed. One provided victory number two for 'Henri' Maltzahn. Another was a first for future Oak Leaves wearer Leutnant Gerhard Michalski of the *Gruppenstab*, while Oberleutnant Heinz Bretnütz (*Kapitän* of 6. *Staffel*) was credited with a brace, which took his score to four. Bretnütz was up on patrol again that evening, when he claimed a Wellington. But although confirmed at the time, this kill is not substantiated by British records.

The winter of 1939/40 was long and harsh. The members of JG 53 whiled away the time on the ground as best they could. In February 1940 a generous blanket of snow was still covering Darmstadt-Griesheim (note the gliding institute's hangar in the background) when Hauptmann Lothar von Janson, *Kommandeur* of I. *Gruppe*, decided to put in a spot of rifle practice, watched by the *Kapitän* of his 2. *Staffel*, Oberleutnant Rolf Pingel

During April it was clear that preparations for the invasion of France were nearing completion. JG 53 began to take delivery of its first, more powerfully armed Bf 109E-4s, and the *Geschwader*'s strength was further bolstered by the temporary attachment of a fourth *Gruppe* – Major Wolf-Heinrich von Houwald's recently formed, and as yet unblooded, III./JG 52, which took up residence at Mannheim-Sandhofen alongside II./JG 53 on 6 April.

In the air, the *Geschwader* was experiencing something of a lull. Another clash with No 73 Sqn's Hurricanes on 7 April resulted in a single kill for 3./JG 53's *Staffelkapitän* Oberleutnant Wolfgang Lippert, who identified his opponent as a Spitfire, but also led to the loss of Feldwebel Erwin Weiss of 4. *Staffel*. Weiss thus had the dubious honour of being the first pilot of JG 53 to fall victim to the RAF, five others having previously been killed in action against the *Armée de l'Air*.

Exactly two weeks later, on 21 April, JG 53 and No 73 Sqn met again. This time Oberleutnant Hans-Karl Mayer had no difficulty in recognising the British fighter he claimed northwest of Merzig as a Hurricane. It was Mayer's second success since taking over from Werner Mölders as *Kapitän* of 1. *Staffel*.

Puzzle picture No 1. With the weak spring sun having finally arrived, and with his work done, the crewchief of 'Yellow 10' grabs the opportunity to doze on the wingroot of his charge. This machine was the usual mount of Oberleutnant Heinz Bretnütz, the *Staffelkapitän* of 6./JG 53 at Mannheim-Sandhofen. On the original print three white kill bars can be made out on the tailfin above the parachute – but Bretnütz's third victim was an MS.406 claimed on the afternoon of 31 March, and his fourth another of the same ilk just two minutes later!

Meanwhile, Mölders himself had been credited with three of the four victories scored by III. *Gruppe* in April 1940. The fourth – another No 73 Sqn Hurricane sent down by Mölders' wingman, Feldwebel Franz Gawlick, near the *Dreiländereck* on 23 April – would prove to be JG 53's last kill of the 'Phoney war'.

Since the British and French declarations of war on 3 September 1939, the *Geschwader* had destroyed 73 enemy aircraft. It had cost the lives of 12 of its pilots – seven killed or missing in action, plus five lost through accidents and other causes.

The experience gained was to stand the unit in good stead in the weeks to come, for when Hitler's forces invaded France and the Low Countries on 10 May 1940 the war suddenly became anything but 'phoney'. And although JG 53 was not always in the forefront of the action during the *Blitzkrieg* in the west, the French campaign enabled II. and I./JG 53 to double and triple their existing scores respectively, while Hauptmann Mölders' III. *Gruppe* was to increase its previous total fivefold.

For the first four days, however, things remained fairly uneventful for the *Geschwader*. While the main focus of attention was centred on the northern flank of the German offensive, where the elaborate 'feint' against Belgium and Holland succeeded in luring British and French troops out of their carefully prepared positions in northeastern France, JG 53's pilots were dividing their time between patrolling the Saarland sector of the Franco-German border – much as they had been doing for the past eight months – and escorting Luftwaffe bombers against targets behind the Maginot Line.

It was not until 14 May that Hitler's true plan of attack became apparent. This was when the Panzer divisions of Army Group A debouched from the leafy valleys of the Ardennes and Eifel Hills – terrain that the French strategists had declared to be 'impassable to tanks'. Having proved the experts wrong, the only major obstacle that now stood between von Rundstedt's armour and the Channel coast was the River Meuse. Once this was crossed, the Panzers could exploit the yawning gap left by the Anglo-French forces' precipitate advance into northern Belgium, split the Allied armies in two and destroy them piecemeal.

Belatedly aware of the looming danger, and recognising the threat posed by the German bridgeheads across the Meuse around Sedan, the French and British threw every bomber they could muster against the river crossings. There was scant time to ensure proper cooperation between the two air arms, however, or to organise adequate and cohesive fighter protection. And so, throughout the daylight hours of 14 May, penny-packets of Allied bombers – some entirely unescorted – were sent in to try to destroy the crossing points. The Messerschmitts were waiting for them.

By the time darkness fell, German pilots on the western front had submitted claims for no fewer than 170(!) enemy machines shot down – the overwhelming majority of them bombers in the area of Sedan. Although this figure is an exaggeration, there is little doubt that the Allied air forces had suffered grievous losses. And 14 May 1940 more than merited its immediate entry into Luftwaffe folklore as the 'Day of the Fighters'.

Having transferred from Darmstadt back up to Kirchberg – the latter by now presumably fully dried out – on the opening day of the *Blitzkrieg*, Hauptmann von Janson's I./JG 53 was to be the most successful of all the *Jagdgeschwader* involved over and around the Sedan bridgeheads. After some inconclusive early morning patrols, the day's action began shortly before noon with the claiming of six French Bloch fighters south of Sedan.

But the greater part of the 35 victories credited to the *Gruppe* on the 'Day of the Fighters' was scored during the main RAF bombing raids on the crossing points in mid-afternoon. In one hectic 35-minute period – when the sky 'seemed full of enemy machines' – von Janson's pilots brought down 20 British Battle and Blenheim bombers, plus a brace of Hurricanes.

The lion's share of the victims – 15 in all – fell to 1./JG 53. This *Staffel* had been ordered to fly a *freie Jagd* sweep to the west of the Meuse, while at the same time providing cover, if necessary, for the Luftwaffe's own outgoing and incoming bomber and Stuka formations. Oberleutnant Hans-Karl Mayer, the *Kapitän* of 1./JG 53, reported;

'The *Staffel* was flying at 5000 metres, passing above a group of Stukas some 1500 metres below us, when we were attacked by six Hurricanes. The top-cover *Schwarm* immediately engaged them. I led the rest of the *Staffel* down to protect the dive-bombers, which were coming under attack from other enemy fighters. I shot down a Hurricane, which crashed and burned on impact.'

In the course of the next 30 minutes, Mayer also accounted for two Battles and two Blenheims, taking his score for the day to five.

During the early evening it was the turn of Oberleutnant Wolfgang Lippert's 3. *Staffel* to make its mark. One of the trio of Blenheims it was

**Puzzle picture No 2. Oberleutnant Hans-Karl Mayer, who had taken over as *Kapitän* of 1./JG 53 after Mölders' departure to set up III. *Gruppe*, poses cheerfully on the tail of his *Emil*, which displays a gaping hole next to the aircraft jacking point. It also has seven kills carefully recorded on the rudder. 'Mayer-Ast' ('Lanky Mayer') was one of the most successful pilots on 14 May 1940 – the 'Day of the Fighters' – when he raised his score from three to eight. And this time a whole 15 minutes was to elapse between victory No 7 (a Blenheim downed at 1640 hrs) and victory No 8 (a Battle claimed at 1655 hrs), both to the south of Sedan**

credited with provided a first for future Oak Leaves centurion Leutnant Wolfgang Tonne. But the four 'Wellingtons' they also claimed were more likely to have been machines of the *Armée de l'Air*.

The performance of the other two *Gruppen* in the Sedan area on this date fell far below that of I./JG 53. Engaged only peripherally, II. *Gruppe* submitted claims for three French fighters, not one of which was allowed. Three of III./JG 53's seven kills were likewise recorded as unconfirmed, leaving it with just a brace of MS.406s to show for its morning's activities, plus a pair of Hurricanes brought down at the height of the RAF's mid-afternoon bombing raids. One of the British fighters took Werner Mölders's score into double figures.

Although JG 53 had been instrumental in enabling the German armour to break out of the Sedan bridgehead, the *Geschwader* would not be following the ground forces' now historic dash across northeastern France to the Channel coast and Dunkirk. Instead, for much of the rest of the month, it would be retained in the Luxembourg-Sedan area flying *freie Jagd* sweeps and bomber escort missions. And while this resulted in few successes for I. and II. *Gruppen*, III./JG 53 went from strength to strength, being credited with nearly 50 enemy aircraft (predominantly French) shot down during the latter half of May.

The victories were not all one-sided, however. On 18 May the *Emils* of 7./JG 53 clashed with eight Curtiss Hawk 75s west of Laon. Two of the French fighters went down, but in the melée the machine of the *Staffelkapitän*, Oberleutnant Wolf-Dietrich Wilcke, was also hit and he was forced to take to his parachute.

*Gruppenkommandeur* Werner Mölders waited four long days in the hope that the *Kapitän* of his 7. *Staffel* had come down in German-held territory, and therefore would return to base, before he reported Wilcke missing and wrote to the latter's stepfather – a general in the artillery – informing him of the fact. But Wilcke, a future *Experte* and Swords recipient had, of course, survived. He had been picked up by the French and taken to Montferrat Castle PoW camp to join other captured Luftwaffe pilots and aircrew.

Nine days after Wilcke's loss, on 27 May, another brief engagement between III./JG 53 and French Hawk 75s – this time to the northwest of Amiens – provided Werner Mölders with his 20th victory of the war.

One of I./JG 53's two fatalities on 14 May was Oberfeldwebel Walter Grimmling – the pilot responsible for the *Geschwader*'s very first victory of the war – who was shot down by RAF Hurricanes. He was initially buried alongside the wreckage of his *Emil*, which crashed at Bouillon, close to the Meuse, downstream from Sedan

Although correctly identified in his logbook at the time as Curtiss Hawks, for some unknown reason Mölders referred to his opponents as 'Bloch fighters' when later describing the action to his biographer.

Flying at the head of 8. *Staffel*, Mölders had spotted the six enemy machines approaching the frontline, and had led his pilots around in a wide curve so as to get behind them. His intention was to gain the element of surprise by attacking the fighters from out of the French hinterland;

'"Everybody close up – attack!" Like a sudden storm we fall upon the completely unsuspecting enemy from above. I line my sights up on the right-hand man of the rear section, Leutnant Panten takes the left, while Leutnant Müller pulls ahead of us and aims for the section leader. Bloch fighters! I can see the blue-white-red stripes on their tails quite clearly – edge in closer, metre by metre, take careful aim, and – right on target! My cannon and machine gun rounds erupt in tiny flashes all over the enemy crate. Another French fighter destroyed!

'All around me my Messerschmitts are doing their job. The second *Schwarm* has overtaken us and is engaging the enemy's leading section. Every Bloch has a '109 glued to its tail. The enemy fighters don't get the chance to fire a single shot. There, Leutnant Kunert's victim is going down in flames. Beneath me I count four explosions as machines hit the ground. The enemy leader is still twisting and turning in confusion. But I keep after him. He too explodes on impact with the ground, not far from where Kunert's opponent went in. The last Frenchman is so shot up by Leutnant Panten that he is forced to belly-land.'

It was all over in little more than 60 seconds. Records indicate that five of the six French fighters were destroyed. The 'Leutnant Müller' referred to by Mölders above was future Oak Leaves winner Friedrich-Karl 'Tutti' Müller. The Curtiss was the first victory of his career. That same afternoon elements of III./JG 53 became embroiled with another, mixed formation of French fighters near Creil. And the outcome was again five *Armée de l'Air* machines downed without loss. Two of the victims, both MS.406 fighters, were the opening entries on the scoresheets of another pair of *Experten*-to-be – Oberfeldwebel Franz Götz and Feldwebel Herbert Schramm.

But it was the second of Mölders' two kills on this 27 May that made all the headlines. The first pilot in the war to achieve a total of 20 enemy aircraft destroyed, he also became the first member of the Luftwaffe to be awarded the Knight's Cross. The prestigious decoration was presented to him by *Generalfeldmarschall* Hermann Göring on 29 May. The hitherto relatively little-known Werner Mölders was suddenly transformed into a national hero. All the more shocking, therefore, was the news received in Germany exactly one week later that he had been reported missing in action.

By that time Operation *Yellow*, the first phase of the Wehrmacht's methodical conquest of France, was complete. The armoured spearheads that had burst out of the Ardennes forests had reached the English Channel. The last British troops had been evacuated from Dunkirk. Northeast France was in German hands. Now the invaders could launch Operation *Red* – the assault against the remaining bulk of the French field armies south of the Rivers Somme and Aisne.

But before supporting the ground operations during this second stage of the *Blitzkrieg* in the west, the Luftwaffe mounted its one major strategic

**Puzzle picture No 3. Hauptmann Werner Mölders proudly wears the Knight's Cross he received for becoming the first pilot to achieve 20 kills in World War 2. The discrepancies in the scores of Bretnütz and Mayer in the photographs on pages 19 and 21 may be the result of differences between claims submitted post-action and claims subsequently confirmed. But Mölders' victories are well documented, so why only 18 on the tailfin of his machine seen here (and it is *his* machine, as the next highest scorer in III. *Gruppe* at the time of the *Kommandeur's* Knight's Cross was Feldwebel Hans Galubinski with just four!)? One suggestion is that this is Mölders's reserve machine, which does not yet display the two kills he achieved northwest of Amiens on 27 May 1940**

bombing raid of the campaign. Flown on 3 June 1940, Operation *Paula* was aimed at the airfields, aircraft manufacturing plants and associated targets in the Greater Paris area. All three of JG 53's *Gruppen* were involved in *Paula*, escorting Do 17 bombers and flying *freie Jagd* missions to the south of the French capital.

The day netted the *Geschwader* a further 14 victories, including two more for Werner Mölders (taking him to 23). But it cost them two pilots – one brought down by French anti-aircraft fire and another by an MS.406.

Operation *Red* began on 5 June. In JG 53's sector however, on the left-hand flank of the offensive, the armoured units of the *Gruppe* Guderian (hitherto XIX. *Panzerkorps*) were not scheduled to advance across the Aisne until 9 June. The *Geschwader* spent the intervening four days primarily flying *freie Jagd* sorties over the area south of the Aisne. And although its pilots encountered relatively little enemy air activity during this period, it was on the first of the four days that III. *Gruppe* was to lose its *Kommandeur*.

Hauptmann Mölders had already taken his score to 25 with a Bloch fighter and a Potez 'twin' claimed near Compiègne shortly before midday on 5 June. Later that same afternoon he took off again for another sweep of the same region. But this time it was the Luftwaffe's foremost ace who was caught unawares. Flying at an altitude of some 760 metres, Mölders had just checked his tail – ''109s twisting and turning all over the place' – but had failed to spot the French Dewoitine D.520 that was bearing down on him. Two brief salvos of fire from the enemy pilot and the *Emil* erupted in flames;

'Suddenly my cockpit was filled with noise and explosions. I almost blacked out! The throttle was shot to pieces, the stick slammed forward and I was going down in a vertical dive – time to get out – otherwise it's all over. I grab the canopy release, the hood flies off and my trusty bird points her nose upwards one last time and gives me the opportunity to release the straps and raise myself out of the seat. Free!'

Mölders drifted to earth about 40 miles inside French-held territory close to an enemy artillery regiment. Despite trying to disappear into the surrounding cornfields, he was quickly rounded up and – like Wolf-Dietrich Wilcke and some half-dozen other members of the *Geschwader* downed by the French – would sit out the remainder of the campaign in enemy captivity.

Unlike Wilcke and the rest, Mölders would not return to JG 53 after release following the French capitulation. He was to spend the early weeks of July on leave, while officially a member of the *Ergänzungsgruppe* Merseburg, before being appointed *Geschwaderkommodore* of JG 51 on 27 July 1940 (see *Osprey Aviation Elite Units 22 – Jagdgeschwader 51 'Mölders'* for further details).

On 9 June – the day General Guderian's Panzers launched their part in Operation *Red* – JG 53 had been ordered to cover the ground forces' advance southwards past Reims. I. and III. *Gruppen* both claimed a trio of French fighters in the Réthel-Reims area without loss to themselves. II./JG 53 was less fortunate. Oberleutnant Otto Böhner, its *Gruppen-TO* (Technical Officer), was forced to bail out after his *Emil* was damaged in a dogfight. Böhner was not only the last member of the *Geschwader* to

Oberleutnant Hans-Karl Mayer (third from left) and pilots of his 1. *Staffel* enjoy the sun at Douzy during the brief hiatus between Operations *Yellow* and *Red* – the two-part conquest of France. The French campaign was very much the calm before the storm for 1./JG 53. Of the six pilots pictured here, only one – Leutnant Ernst-Albrecht Schultz, to the right of Mayer – would still be with the *Staffel* by the end of the Battle of Britain. The other five had all been either killed or captured in the seven weeks from late August to mid-October 1940

suffer temporary French captivity – he was also its last combat casualty of the entire campaign.

During the course of the next 48 hours, III./JG 53, under acting-*Kommandeur* Hauptmann Rolf Pingel, was credited with a further ten French fighters destroyed south of the Aisne. These were to be the *Geschwader*'s final successes of the *Blitzkrieg* in the west. The remaining fortnight of the campaign saw little activity for the pilots of JG 53. On 20 June III. *Gruppe* was tasked with providing a fighter umbrella above the forest of Compiègne, where German and French representatives were beginning negotiations for an armistice. And on the day the armistice was signed, 22 June, JG 53's units received orders to vacate the fields they had been occupying along the River Marne, east of Paris and transfer westwards into Brittany.

Here, based at Rennes (*Stab*, I. and III. *Gruppen*) and Dinan (II. *Gruppe*), JG 53 was to be responsible for guarding the coastline of northwestern France.

With the ceasefire in France coming into effect at 0035 hrs on 25 June, it was clear that the next stage of the hostilities would involve taking the war across the Channel to Great Britain. It was equally obvious that any such undertaking would be concentrated along the narrowest stretch of the Channel opposite southeast England.

Having been only peripherally involved on the extreme left-hand flank of operations during much of the recent fighting in France, it appeared that the 'Ace of Spades' – now ordered to defend the westernmost and widest sector of the English Channel where it opened out onto the Atlantic Ocean – was again about to be sidelined in the forthcoming Battle of Britain.

# THE BATTLE OF BRITAIN AND BEYOND

The opening phase of the Battle of Britain only served to underline JG 53's isolation from the main scene of operations. The Luftwaffe's first objective was to deny the English Channel to British shipping, and this was far more likely to be achieved along the narrower eastern end of the Channel, and in the 21-mile width of the Straits of Dover, than across the almost 100 miles of open water separating Brittany from the coasts of Devon and Cornwall.

Having been rushed up into Brittany even before the fighting in France had officially ceased, the *Geschwader*'s 120 *Emils* then spent all of July fruitlessly guarding this northwestern corner of the newly conquered country against raids that never materialised.

As the month progressed, RAF Bomber Command began to focus its efforts almost exclusively on attacking Luftwaffe airfields and the concentrations of invasion barges being gathered in the ports of northeast France and the Low Countries.

It was not until the second week of August that JG 53 finally entered the fray. As the *Geschwader*'s bases at Rennes and Dinan were too far south to allow its short-legged Bf 109s to operate effectively over England, the unit was assigned airfields in the Channel Islands and around Cherbourg, on the tip of the Cotentin Peninsula, to use as forward landing grounds, or jumping-off points, for cross-Channel sorties. But even these fields did not permit their venturing too far inland over enemy territory.

Most of the fighting during JG 53's first fortnight of the Battle would, therefore, be restricted to the coastal belt of Dorset and the waters off the Isle of Wight. In fact, it had already flown several exploratory sweeps over these areas at the end of July, but without result. It was the Luftwaffe's

The Battle of Britain began quietly enough for JG 53, which was tasked with the coastal defence of northwest France. The almost total lack of enemy air activity in the area gave Hauptleute Rolf Pingel (left) and Hans-Karl Mayer, the *Kapitäne* of 2. and 1. *Staffeln* respectively, ample time to fool for the camera

Most of the *Geschwader*'s early operations over the western Channel were staged out of either Cherbourg or the Channel Islands. At Villiaze, on Guernsey, its *Emils* were refuelled with the aid of one of Mr J H Miller's Commer trucks (the vehicle has presumably not been officially requisitioned, as it still bears its civilian number plate)

all-out attempt to sink every single ship of convoy CW 9 that was to result in JG 53's first confrontation with the RAF's defending fighters.

The 20-ship convoy, codenamed *Peewit*, had sailed from the Thames Estuary late on 7 August. The following day, as it battled westwards along the Channel, it was subjected to a series of fierce surface and air attacks from E-boats and Stukas. By late afternoon, the survivors were off the Isle of Wight. And it was here that they were subjected to yet another dive-bombing assault, this time by Ju 87s of II./StG 77, part of whose escort was provided by Hauptmann Günther von Maltzahn's II./JG 53 up from Villiaze, on Guernsey.

While the Stukas hurled themselves upon the convoy, sinking four ships, damaging seven, and scattering the remainder, II./JG 53 engaged its four-squadron strong fighter screen. After ten minutes of violent skirmishing south of Swanage, the *Emils* were forced to break off and head back to Guernsey. They had claimed a Hurricane and two Spitfires, the second of which took the score of Hauptmann Heinz Bretnütz, the *Kapitän* of 6. *Staffel*, into double figures. These were the *Geschwader*'s first successes for almost two months.

Heavy cloud over the Channel restricted operations for the next 48 hours, but on 11 August the Luftwaffe mounted its largest raid yet against Britain when it despatched a mixed force of Ju 88 and He 111 bombers to attack the naval base at Portland. The fighter screen included all three of JG 53's *Gruppen* and – despite the strength of the opposition, from which its pilots claimed eight Spitfires destroyed – they again returned to base without loss. Among III. *Gruppe*'s five kills were a trio for its recently appointed *Kommandeur*, Hauptmann Harro Harder, an 11-victory veteran of the *Legion Condor*.

Shortly after arriving back at Dinan (via Villiaze) later that same afternoon, Leutnant Erich Bodendiek of 4. *Staffel* added a ninth to the day's collective score by chasing and bringing down what was described as a 'reconnaissance Blenheim' close to the French coast.

So far the *Geschwader* had borne a charmed life in its encounters with RAF Fighter Command. That was to change on 12 August when all three *Gruppen* were again involved in action off the Isle of Wight during a series of *freie Jagd* sweeps. Although I. and III./JG 53 were credited with four enemy fighters apiece, the latter then suffered the 'Ace of Spades'' first combat fatality of the Battle. This was their new *Kommandeur*, Hauptmann Harro Harder, who was heard over the R/T reporting the destruction of two Hurricanes (claims that were to remain unconfirmed due to lack of witnesses) before he was himself shot down into the sea somewhere off the coast of Dorset.

Hauptmann Wolf-Dietrich Wilcke, the *Kapitän* of 7. *Staffel*, was immediately named as Harder's replacement, and only narrowly escaped joining his predecessor on the casualty list just a few hours later. It was during another sortie that same afternoon that Wilcke's *Emil* sustained engine damage – whether from enemy action or not is unclear – and he was forced to bail out over the Channel. Having already taken to his parachute once before, and survived a spell in French captivity, Wilcke was again fortunate in that there was a bright moon that evening. He was spotted and picked up by the air-sea rescue (ASR) flying-boat sent out to search for him.

On 13 August the Luftwaffe was finally given the go-ahead to launch *'Adlertag', or* 'Eagle Day'. But due to a combination of bad weather and poor communications, this long-awaited major assault – intended to administer the *coup de grâce* to the RAF – descended into chaos and confusion.

JG 53's opening contributions to the day's proceedings consisted of abortive cross-Channel *freie Jagd* sorties flown above almost solid cloud. Then, shortly before midday, II. and III. *Gruppen* each claimed an intruding Blenheim close to their home bases. Late in the afternoon I. and II./JG 53 again headed out over the Channel, this time accompanying a Stuka raid on Portland. Although the Ju 87s of II./StG 1 were beaten by the weather and turned back before reaching their target, JG 53's two *Gruppen* became entangled in a succession of bitter dogfights with Spitfires and Hurricanes in the Portland area.

When it was all over I. and II./JG 53 had, between them, been credited with nine enemy fighters destroyed. But they had lost four of their own pilots (one killed and three captured), all from II. *Gruppe*. And unlike those who had been taken into temporary captivity during the French campaign three months earlier, all pilots shot down in the course of the battle over England – and this would ultimately include some 30 from the ranks of JG 53 alone – were effectively lost to the Luftwaffe for good (unless, that is, they were so badly wounded that they were repatriated back to Germany at a later date, as was to happen to two of the three members of JG 53 taken prisoner on 'Eagle Day').

The *Geschwader* saw further action over the Portland and Isle of Wight areas during the next four days, and its pilots could not understand how the RAF's fighters always seemed to be ready and waiting for them – 'they invariably bounced us from above out of the sun!', pilots routinely

Machines of 5./JG 53 taxi out for a massed take-off from Cherbourg at the start of another cross-Channel sortie sometime in August 1940

reported. Apparently unaware at first of the role being played by Britain's radar defences and ground-control organisations, JG 53's pilots were convinced that there was an undiscovered telephone link still operating between the Channel Islands and the United Kingdom. 'At any rate, the *Engländer* always had prior knowledge of our approach, and they were expecting us – even if we flew in at wave-top height and didn't begin to climb until just before the coast'.

Somebody higher up the chain of command was slightly better informed, however, for on 18 August I./JG 53 was ordered to escort a *Stukagruppe* in a raid on Poling radar station to the east of the Isle of Wight. Although I./JG 53 lost only one of its charges, and was able to down three British fighters, other dive-bombers attacking targets nearby received a savage mauling at the hands of the RAF. So grievous were the losses, in fact, that 18 August marked the virtual end of the once seemingly invincible Stukas in the daylight skies of northwest Europe. Shortly afterwards they were transferred up into the Pas de Calais area, where they sat out the rest of the Battle in idleness, waiting for the call to support the ground campaign in southern England that never happened.

The disappearance of the Stukas coincided with a new phase of the Battle. Hitherto, the Luftwaffe's aerial onslaught had been carried out on a broad front, along almost the entire length of the Channel. This lack of concentration on any one particular area had proven ineffective and costly. At a conference on 19 August *Reichsmarschall* Göring therefore decreed that the major effort was to be directed against southeast England and the regions around London. And in order to provide the strongest possible fighter escorts for the planned armadas of bombers earmarked for this offensive, nearly all the Bf 109 *Gruppen* currently stationed under *Luftflotte* 3 in northwest France were also to be moved to the Pas de Calais and placed under the control of *Luftflotte* 2.

Among the *Geschwader* involved in the transfer was JG 53, whose *Gruppen* were assigned a clutch of airfields along the French coast south of Cap Gris Nez. The first to make the move was Oberstleutnant von Cramon's *Geschwaderstab*, which flew into Etaples on 23 August. III./JG 53 was ordered to Le Touquet 24 hours later, but not before making one last visit to its old stamping grounds by escorting a formation of He 111s to Portland in the early evening of 25 August that resulted in the shooting down of three Spitfires.

The other two *Gruppen* were also active in the west right up until the moment of transfer. On 24 August they too had, between them, claimed three Spitfires (off the Isle of Wight). The next day proved to be one of the most successful of the whole Battle for I./JG 53, with its pilots being credited with no fewer than eight Hurricanes destroyed in the Portland area against the loss of a single pilot who forced-landed and was captured.

One of the eight fighters was victory number 15 for the *Kapitän* of 1./JG 53, Hauptmann Hans-Karl Mayer, who had been the third pilot in the *Geschwader* to take his score into double figures a fortnight earlier. Mayer's combat report for 25 August was the usual model of brevity;

'Mission – *freie Jagd* during a bombing raid on Portland. The *Staffel* engaged a *Staffel* of Hurricanes that was attempting to get at the Ju 88s. I got on the tail of a Hurricane that was shooting at a Ju 88 from a great distance. It then broke off and dived away northwest towards the coast.

The unmistakable figure of Hans-Karl Mayer towers over members of his 1. *Staffel* groundcrew, all of whom appear to be studying something of interest in the area of the starboard tailplane. The last two of the 17 kill bars marked on the rudder of the *Kapitän's Emil* refer to the brace of Spitfires downed near Portsmouth on 26 August

I dived after it and shot the machine in flames from a range of 50 metres. After another burst of machine-gun fire from just ten metres away, the pilot bailed out. Machine and pilot fell into the water 500 metres off the coast.'

Mayer's opponent, a Belgian volunteer flying for the RAF, did not survive the encounter. His body was washed ashore three days later.

II. *Gruppe* got a brace of Spitfires during this same mission covering the withdrawal of the Luftwaffe bombers, but it cost the unit two missing and two brought down wounded into the Channel, both of whom were picked up by their own ASR service.

The two *Gruppen* flew another combined *freie Jagd* operation, this time in the Portsmouth area, the following day, 26 August. Again, II./JG 53 came off worse. Unable to score a single kill, it lost two pilots over the Channel, while a third was fished out of the sea north of Cherbourg. By contrast, I. *Gruppe* were credited with four Spitfires on this date, including two for Hans-Karl Mayer, but only at the expense of one pilot killed when his *Emil* suffered engine failure and crashed near Portsmouth.

On 28 August I.and II./JG 53 then departed Brittany for their new bases in the Pas de Calais, taking up residence at Neuville and Sempy, respectively.

For the past three weeks or more the engine cowlings of every one of JG 53's machines had been sporting a red band that was just wide enough to completely obliterate the unit's distinctive 'Ace of Spades' insignia. The official reason given for the adoption of this marking, which dated back to an order issued in late July, was that it was an intelligence subterfuge. The 'Ace of Spades' had become too well known to the RAF. And the sudden appearance of the 'Red stripe' unit was to fool the enemy into believing that an entirely new *Jagdgeschwader* had been added to the Luftwaffe's Channel front order of battle.

At first the 'red band' edict was scrupulously complied with. Future *Experte* and Oak Leaves winner Gerhard Michalski, currently the *Gruppen-Adjutant* of II./JG 53, is pictured in front of the machine flown by his *Kommandeur*, Hauptmann Günther von Maltzahn. The freshly applied unit marking, completely encircling the engine cowling, is clearly visible

But the red band did not remain intact for long. This I. *Gruppe Emil* being pushed into its sandbagged and camouflage-netted dispersal bay has obviously had its yellow cowling replaced, leaving the red around the lower panel only . . .

But according to most historians, the change was introduced not out of operational necessity, but as a result of personal antagonism. It was no secret that by this time the *Geschwaderkommodore*, Oberstleutnant Hans-Jürgen von Cramon-Taubadel, had become very much *persona non grata* within the Luftwaffe hierarchy – not least because he had chosen to marry a lady who was, in his own words, 'not wholly Aryan'. The red band was thus regarded as a snub to his command of the 'Ace of Spades'.

If this was indeed the case, it was not the only injustice suffered by von Cramon. Unlike many of his World War 1 contemporaries who commanded *Jagd-* and *Zerstörergeschwader* in 1940 – the likes of Harry von Bülow-Bothkamp, Joachim-Friedrich Huth, Max Ibel and Theo Osterkamp – he was never awarded the Knight's Cross. And he was to remain under something of a cloud for the rest of his Luftwaffe career, being shunted off to the backwaters of Scandinavia to serve as chief-of-staff to various local commands during the later years of the war. Perhaps not entirely by chance, it was not until after he had relinquished command of JG 53 (some considerable time thereafter, in fact – the powers-that-be did not want to make the connection too obvious!) that the 'Ace of Spades' was reinstated on the *Geschwader's* fighters.

. . . whereas this machine in a rudimentary revetment at Le Touquet – starting handle in place, but no bomb yet attached to that ventral rack – has had the reverse treatment, boasting a replacement lower engine panel with the red band around the upper cowling only. As a supposedly 'new' unit marking the red band was hardly likely to fool RAF intelligence, as formations were soon displaying a bewildering array of red bands, partial red bands, or no red bands at all – see, for example, the earlier illustration of 5. *Staffel* taking off from Cherbourg on page 28

The pilots had reacted to this sorry episode in their unit's history in different ways. One expressed his indignation by painting a large question mark on the red band where the 'Ace of Spades' used to be. Others used the subsequent introduction of all-yellow cowlings – a bona fide Channel front recognition marking – as an excuse to overpaint the red band. III./JG 53 did not seek any excuse. Commanded by Hauptmann Wolf-Dietrich Wilcke, himself no ardent supporter of the Berlin Regime, its pilots responded to the disappearance of their badge

by simply painting out the swastikas on their tailfins, and using the space thus made available to record their individual scores.

But these undercurrents were not allowed to interfere with operations. Based in the Pas de Calais, JG 53 now found itself involved in a somewhat different type of campaign from that which it had been conducting in the west. Gone were the long overwater flights and the freebooting *freie Jagd* missions around the Isle of Wight. Its main duty henceforth would be to protect the massed bomber formations attacking targets in southeast England.

Despite the more rigid flying discipline this imposed upon the Bf 109E pilots (the bomber crews liked to see their fighter cover in close proximity and, by express order of the *Reichsmarschall*, those *Jagdgruppen* assigned to close escort had to provide exactly that), JG 53 continued to maintain a very creditable kill-to-loss ratio. During the first week of September it was credited with close on 30 RAF aircraft destroyed for the loss of 11 pilots killed, missing or captured.

But when the Luftwaffe turned its full attention on London – starting with a heavy daylight raid on the capital on 7 September – the 'Ace of Spades'' losses began to rise. By the time the month was out five of the *Geschwader*'s nine *Staffelkapitäne* (including all three of III. *Gruppe*) would have been killed.

The bomber traffic was not all one-way, however. Although the pilots of RAF Fighter Command were – and still are – rightfully lionised for bearing the full brunt of the defensive battle, the efforts of Bomber and Coastal Commands during the summer and early autumn of 1940 sometimes tend to get overlooked. Yet their actions were no less heroic as they sought, often against impossible odds, to take the war back across the Channel to German-occupied Europe by bombing Luftwaffe airfields and the ever-growing numbers of invasion vessels still gathering in the Channel ports.

The distinctly tatty yellow cowling of 7. *Staffel*'s captured 'White 5' bears no sign of a red band, nor of a swastika on the tailfin. The latter has clearly been overpainted, which was III. *Gruppe*'s collective response to the loss of the 'Ace of Spades' *Geschwader* badge. Most pilots utilised the space thus made available to display their scoreboard. But if, as is believed, this is the 'White 5' put down on its belly near Manston on 6 September by Unteroffizier Hans-Georg Schulte, he has made no attempt to record his six previous kills (a seventh was credited to him during his final mission)

But all this talk of red bands detracts from the real significance and cost of the Battle of Britain, which resulted in the Luftwaffe suffering its first reversal of the war. JG 53 bore its fair share of the casualties. Representative of the many, now largely unknown, young pilots lost was 2. *Staffel*'s Rudolf Schmid, seen here as a leutnant enjoying something long and refreshing during the campaign in France, where he claimed his only two victories. Oberleutnant Schmid was one of the three pilots of JG 53 killed on 15 September 1940 – 'Battle of Britain Day' – shot down by a No 603 Sqn Spitfire over Maidstone

It was while returning from yet another bomber escort mission to London late in the afternoon of 11 September that Hauptmann Wolf-Dietrich Wilcke's III./JG 53 encountered one such raiding force – apparently a mixed formation of biplane and monoplane bombers – that had been sent to attack Calais. Wilcke and two of his pilots each claimed one of the biplanes, which they simply described as *Doppldecker* (their unfamiliarity with the type was perhaps excusable – the first few Fairey Albacores had only been in Fleet Air Arm service for some six months). The *Gruppe* was also credited with two Blenheims shot down over Calais, although these were not bombers but Blenheim IVF fighters of No 235 Sqn flying cover for the naval machines.

Then came 15 September, the date now celebrated annually as Battle of Britain Day. It witnessed the Luftwaffe's last major daylight bombing raids on London. Altogether, close on 1100 individual sorties were flown that day, the vast majority of them in the two main attacks against the English capital. All three of JG 53's *Gruppen* were involved in both operations, but with markedly different degrees of success.

Despite a number of clashes with RAF fighters, Hauptmann Günther von Maltzahn's II./JG 53 had neither claims nor losses to show for its day's activities. I. *Gruppe*, on the other hand, was credited with nine enemy fighters – four Spitfires, including a pair for *Kommandeur* Hauptmann Hans-Karl Mayer shortly after midday, and a mixed bag of Spitfires and Hurricanes during its second foray to London later that same afternoon. These victories did not come cheaply, however, as six pilots had failed to return. Three were killed and the others shot down and captured.

But it was *'Fürst'* ('Prince') Wilcke's III./JG 53 that was the most successful of all on 15 September. Its score for the day of 11 machines destroyed – again including a brace of Spitfires for the *Kommandeur* – had been achieved for the loss of just two *Emils* (one down in the Channel and the second crash-landing in France), both of whose pilots survived unhurt.

The *Gruppe* had been credited with bringing down six Spitfires during its early afternoon mission to London, plus a further three – together with a single Hurricane – during the subsequent raid. Its eleventh, and final, success of the day, a Blenheim claimed by future Knight's Cross recipient Feldwebel Hermann Neuhoff over the Channel between Cap Gris Nez and Le Touquet at 1700 hrs, remains something of a mystery. No Blenheim was lost in action on Battle of Britain Day, but 20 minutes after Neuhoff's reported kill, a Bristol Beaufighter (a type newly introduced into service with No 25 Sqn) crashed near Biggin Hill for reasons that are unknown. Could this have been Neuhoff's victim, damaged over the Channel and attempting to get back to its North Weald base?

Although a number of individual units, III./JG 53 included, performed well on 15 September 1940, the Luftwaffe's overall 'defeat' on this date – i.e. its obvious failure to deliver the final knock-out blow to RAF Fighter Command – marked the beginning of the end of the Battle. Göring revised his tactics yet again, reducing the size of his bomber formations, and providing them with maximum fighter escort, while Hitler postponed Operation *Seelöwe* ('Sealion'), the planned invasion of southern England, until further notice.

During the latter half of September, the 'Ace of Spades' pilots accounted for three-dozen RAF fighters, while losing just one of their own

Pilots of 3. *Staffel* pose for a snapshot to 'celebrate' their new role as *Jabo* specialists. The bomb bears the inscription 'The 3rd greets London'. Standing at the extreme right is *Kapitän* Oberleutnant Walter Rupp who, on 17 October, would also end his operational career with a belly-landing at Manston. Next to him, hands in pockets, is future centurion, and Oak Leaves recipient, Wolfgang Tonne

killed, two missing and four captured. Among the successes was the first of the war for the *Geschwaderstab*, although the Hurricane claimed by the *Kommodore* south of Ashford in Kent on 27 September was, in fact, the second on his personal score sheet – he had opened with a MS.406 back in December 1939 when serving as *Gruppenkommandeur* of I./JG 54.

Three days later, on 30 September, Oberstleutnant Hans-Jürgen von Cramon-Taubadel – he of the 'not entirely Aryan' wife – relinquished command of JG 53 to take up the first of a long succession of staff postings. The officer selected to replace von Cramon was Major Günther von Maltzahn, previously the *Kommandeur* of II. *Gruppe*, who would remain at the head of the *Geschwader* for the next three years. And II./JG 53's highest scorer, the 17-victory Hauptmann Heinz Bretnütz, *Staffelkapitän* of 6./JG 53, was in turn moved up to take over from von Maltzahn as *Gruppenkommandeur*.

**A yellow-nosed Bf 109E-4/B of 3./JG 53, all bombed-up and ready to go, at Le Touquet in October 1940**

By early October the Luftwaffe's bombers were resorting more and more to the hours of darkness to carry out their raids on Great Britain. And in order to retain some semblance of a daylight offensive, it was at this juncture that Göring ordered a third of all his fighters to be converted to the *Jabo*, or fighter-bomber, role. A *Staffel* from each of von Maltzahn's three *Gruppen* were selected to undergo modification. Those chosen were 3., 4. and 8./JG 53.

Thus, having initially flown *freie Jagd* sweeps over the Isle of Wight area, and then carried out bomber escort duties against London, the pilots of JG 53 would be primarily employed during the dying days of the Battle providing fighter cover for their own three *Jabostaffeln*, as well as for the dedicated Bf 109E fighter-bombers of II.(*Schl*)/LG 2.

While so doing, they continued to claim a steady, if diminishing, toll of RAF fighters, some 25 enemy machines being added to the *Geschwader*'s collective total during the course of October. But their own losses were now rising disproportionately. In the same period six pilots were killed, two reported missing, and six shot down and captured. The highest number of casualties in men and machines was suffered by the *Jabostaffeln*, and included all three *Staffelkapitäne*. This was perhaps not surprising, as none of the *Staffeln* had been withdrawn from operations for even the most rudimentary of training in their new role. They had had to learn the specialised techniques of fighter-bombing while 'on the job', and not always with the most satisfactory of results.

But October's most grievous loss was undoubtedly that of Hauptmann Hans-Karl Mayer, the *Gruppenkommandeur* of I./JG 53. The *Geschwader*'s current highest scorer (with 22 victories) and only serving Knight's Cross holder, Mayer had been forced to abort a mission on 17 October and return early to base with a damaged engine. Back at Le Touquet, he immediately ordered another machine made ready. Unfortunately, the only one available was a newly-delivered E-7, which had not yet been armed, whose radio was not properly tuned and which lacked a dinghy. He nonetheless took this up on what he described as a 'test-flight' after learning that his senior *Staffelkapitän* had also had to turn back with a mechanical defect, and that his depleted and virtually leaderless force was already being heavily engaged by RAF fighters to the east of London.

Nothing more was heard from Hans-Karl Mayer. It seems fairly certain, however, that once aloft he had decided to head north in his unarmed *Emil* to try to find his embattled *Gruppe*. References differ as to what may have happened next. At least one maintains that he fell victim to RAF Spitfires over the Thames Estuary (as had Oberleutnant Walter Rupp, the *Kapitän* of 3. *Staffel*, who belly-landed his damaged fighter-bomber at Manston).

The only thing known with certainty is that Hauptmann Mayer's body was washed ashore north of Dungeness ten days later. In the interim, the *Gruppe* had been led temporarily by Oberleutnant Ignaz Prestele, *Staffelkapitän* of 2./JG 53, until Mayer's official replacement, Hauptmann Hans-Heinrich Brustellin, was posted in from I./JG 51.

It was at this time, too, that the *Geschwader* was honoured with its third Knight's Cross of the war. The unidentified (and, truth be told,

**Among the first of the six *Geschwader* pilots to enter British captivity in October was another *Jabo Staffelkapitän*, Oberleutnant Walter Fiel of 8./JG 53, who belly-landed near Tunbridge on 2 October. His 'Black 7' was subsequently put on display in Sunderland, where the intricacies of its Daimler-Benz engine are being explained to an enthralled female audience by a member of the local Home Guard**

**Seen wearing his Knight's Cross – the second won by the *Geschwader* after Mölders' award back in May – Hauptmann Hans-Karl Mayer, *Gruppenkommandeur* of I./JG 53, was lost in unknown circumstances on 17 October 1940**

Mayer's temporary replacement as acting-*Kommandeur* of I. *Gruppe* was Oberleutnant Ignaz Prestele, the *Staffelkapitän* of 2./JG 53, pictured here in his 'Black 2' under a screen of camouflage netting at Le Touquet as he and his mechanic await the order to start engines

One of a series of propaganda photographs purportedly taken to mark Oberfeldwebel Stefan Litjens' scoring JG 53's 500th kill of the war on 15 November 1940 (although post-war records cast serious doubt on both total and date as given), this shot nonetheless shows a gathering of future *Experten* who, between them, would add nearly 250 victories to the 'Ace of Spades'' collective score. In the foreground an ebullient 'Steff' Litjens (left) receives a congratulatory handshake from Franz Götz. To the rear (from left to right) are Kurt Brändle, Heinz Bretnütz (partially obscured by Götz), Wolf-Dietrich Wilcke and Erich Schmidt

somewhat suspect) Hurricane claimed by Hauptmann Heinz Bretnütz on the afternoon of 20 October had taken his score to 20. The recently appointed *Gruppenkommandeur* of II./JG 53 was presented with his award 48 hours later.

For the remainder of the month, weather permitting, JG 53 continued to fly two, and sometimes three, missions a day – mostly escorted fighter-bomber raids on the Greater London area. Such levels of activity played havoc with the *Geschwader*'s already precarious serviceability figures, and by the beginning of November it was operating at less than half establishment strength. The situation deteriorated further as November progressed. In fact, with the onset of winter weather the day-light battle as a whole was rapidly winding down, and JG 53 was not alone in experiencing a sharp reduction in operational activity.

I. *Gruppe*, for example, did not achieve a single further kill after the Spitfire claimed southeast of London by Leutnant Wolfgang Tonne on 17 October – the day Hauptmann Hans-Karl Mayer had been reported missing. III./JG 53 was credited with three RAF machines destroyed during the course of November, but these were offset by an equal number of losses. Only II. *Gruppe* ended its part in the Battle with more of a bang than a whimper. Its 18 November victories (achieved at a cost of five pilots lost) included a further half-dozen for *Kommandeur* Hauptmann Heinz Bretnütz – taking him to 26 overall – plus successes for future *Experten* Kurt Brändle, Stefan Litjens and Gerhard Michalski, all of whose scores were as yet still in single figures.

JG 53's final victory of 1940 went, perhaps fittingly, to Major Günther von Maltzahn. The Hurricane he claimed on 1 December – his second since assuming command of the *Geschwader* – raised his score to 12. And the following day was to witness the unit's last combat loss of the year when 1. *Staffel's* Leutnant Fischer was reported missing after a fight with Spitfires off Dungeness.

The 'Ace of Spades" role in the Battle of Britain, like that in the Battle of France which had preceded it, could best be described as useful

rather than spectacular. It came to an end during the week before Christmas 1940 when the entire *Geschwader* returned to Germany to rest and refit. Over the next three months, based in and around the Cologne region, its losses were made good and the unit underwent conversion to the new Bf 109F.

After filtering back to the French Channel coast during March and early April 1941, JG 53's three *Gruppen* resumed their offensive against the RAF. But there was little sense of urgency, and no signs whatsoever of

One result of Major Günther *Freiherr* von Maltzahn's appointment as *Kommodore* in October was the reinstatement of the *Geschwader's* famous badge the following month. Here, 'Henri' von Maltzahn (left) oversees the stencilling of the iconic 'Ace of Spades' on his yellow-nosed *Emil*

Displaying its newly applied badge, the *Kommodore's* machine provides a fitting backdrop to a line-up of some of the *Geschwader's* leading pilots pictured at Etaples in November. They are, from left to right, Leutnant Ernst Klager (7. *Staffel*), Oberleutnant Kurt Brändle (*Staffelkapitän* 5. *Staffel*), Hauptmann Wolf-Dietrich Wilcke (*Gruppenkommandeur* III. *Gruppe*), Major von Maltzahn (*Kommodore*), Hauptmann Heinz Bretnütz (*Gruppenkommandeur* II. *Gruppe*), Oberfeldwebel Stefan Litjens (4. *Staffel*), Hauptmann Hans-Heinrich Brustellin (*Gruppenkommandeur* I. *Gruppe*), Leutnant Erich Schmidt (9. *Staffel*) and Oberleutnant Franz Götz (*Staffelkapitän* 9. *Staffel*)

The *Stabsrotte* (two-aircraft element) of III./JG 53 taxies out at Le Touquet at the start of another mission early in December. The machine of *Gruppen-Adjutant* Leutnant Erich Schmidt in the foreground carries 17 kill bars, while that of his *Kommandeur*, Hauptmann Wolf-Dietrich Wilcke, beyond, displays 13. Schmidt's *Emil* wears the early style, narrow-bordered fuselage crosses still to be seen on many III. *Gruppe* aircraft right up until the end of 1940. Note too that although the 'Ace of Spades' is clearly in evidence again, neither machine has yet had its tailfin swastika restored

any preparations for the seaborne invasion postponed from the previous autumn. Instead, the *Geschwader*'s new *Friedrichs* were employed primarily on a series of desultory *freie Jagd* sweeps and in providing fighter escort for the Luftwaffe's limited number of specialised *Jabostaffeln* now attacking targets along England's southern coast.

These operations did not achieve a great deal of success. The *Kommodore*, Major von Maltzahn, was able to add three more Spitfires to his personal score in March and April, but I. *Gruppe* managed just one single kill during its second stint on the Channel front when Wolfgang Tonne – who had been credited with I./JG 53's final victory in 1940 back in October – claimed a Spitfire south of Boulogne on 26 April.

III. *Gruppe* fared a little better with five confirmed kills, all scored over the Straits of Dover area during May. Only II./JG 53 marked its return to the Channel with a collective score running into double figures. Among the 16 RAF machines its pilots downed between March and May 1941 were five for *Gruppenkommandeur* Hauptmann Heinz Bretnütz and five for future Channel front *Experte*, and posthumous Swords recipient, Feldwebel Josef Wurmheller (see *Osprey Aviation Elite Units 1 - Jagdgeschwader 2 'Richthofen'* for further details).

JG 53's overall tally of 25 enemy aircraft destroyed during the spring of 1941 may not have been unduly impressive, but it far outweighed its own operational losses of one pilot missing, one captured and four wounded. In fact, more casualties and material damage were suffered as a result of accidents during this time than were sustained in combat. Furthermore, its opponents were no longer fighting with their backs to the wall as they had been doing for much of the latter half of 1940.

1 *Staffel*'s Oberleutnant Hans Ohly dons an early pattern kapok life-jacket in preparation for another cross-Channel sortie in his brand new BF 109 at Crecy in April 1941

The RAF's famous 'lean into France' of summer 1941 had not yet begun in earnest, but Bomber Command Blenheims were already striking at coastal targets, including Luftwaffe airfields. On 16 April 1941, for example, seven *Friedrichs* of III. *Gruppe* were damaged to varying degree in one such early 'Circus' operation against Berck-sur-Mer south of Le Touquet. Oddly, although the pair of Spitfires that 7./JG 53's Leutnant Herbert Schramm claimed over the Straits on this date remained unconfirmed – presumably from lack of witnesses – they may well have been the two Polish-flown machines of No 303 Sqn that formed part of the Blenheims' escort, and which were shot down off Dungeness.

Twenty-four hours earlier, on 15 April, II. *Gruppe* had had insult added to injury when its base at St Omer Arques had been ground strafed – by Messerschmitts of JG 52, whose pilots were convinced that they were flying over southern England! The two members of 4./JG 53 injured in the attack, including *Staffelkapitän* Oberleutnant Kurt Liedke, accounted for exactly half of those 'wounded in action' during the spring of 1941.

As May drew to a close it was obvious that there was going to be no cross-Channel invasion. The *Führer* had his sights on a new enemy. Ignoring the advice of his generals, who were only too well aware of the risks involved in waging a two-front war, Hitler was now intent on attacking the Soviet Union.

As part of the Luftwaffe force scheduled to take part in the assault on Russia, JG 53 turned its back on the French Channel coast for good early in June 1941 and returned to Germany, where the unit would spend a few days at its home bases at Mannheim-Sandhofen and Wiesbaden-Erbenheim, making final preparations for the war in the east.

**Although already showing obvious signs of wear, this *Friedrich*, the mount of Hauptmann Heinz Bretnütz, *Kommandeur* of II. *Gruppe*, can still arouse a certain amount of interest – or is that concern? – as it warms up at St Omer Arques in the spring of 1941. It was in this machine – see colour profile 13 – that 'Pietsch' Bretnütz forced-landed on the opening day of *Barbarossa*. It was later recovered, repaired and sent to a training unit, where the veteran fighter was finally written off in a crash late in 1942**

# *BARBAROSSA* AND BEYOND

During their time on the eastern front, JG 53's three *Gruppen* operated completely independently of each other. For the sake of clarity, it is therefore best to chronicle each *Gruppe's* activities in Russia consecutively and on a similarly individual basis.

Operation *Barbarossa*, the invasion of the Soviet Union, was launched along three main fronts, or sectors – north, centre and south. Each sector had its own attached *Luftflotte*, or air fleet, to support land operations.

Major von Maltzahn's *Stab* JG 53, together with I. *Gruppe* – commanded since the departure of Hauptmann Brustellin on 31 March by Oberleutnant Wilfried Balfanz – were assigned to *Luftflotte* 2 in the central sector. They had departed Mannheim-Sandhofen on 14 June 1941 for Krzewica, a landing ground in occupied Poland close to the Soviet border west of Brest-Litovsk. This placed von Maltzahn's units (which also included the attached IV./JG 51) on the right-hand flank of Army Group Centre. Their main task would be to support the armoured divisions of *Panzergruppe* 2 as they advanced along the northern edge of the Pripyet Marshes towards the town of Bobruisk.

But first, *Barbarossa*. Like every other *Blitzkrieg* campaign that had preceded it, the offensive would open with pre-emptive air strikes on the enemy's frontline airfields. I./JG 53's war in the east began at 0340 hrs on the morning of 22 June 1941 when its pilots took off in the half light before dawn to escort the first of a series of Stuka raids in the Brest-Litovsk area.

Caught completely unawares, the Soviets offered no aerial opposition to this initial strike. It was a different matter later in the day, however, as the Red Air Force slowly began to respond to the German assault. At first, Oberleutnant Balfanz's pilots merely encountered the occasional Red Air Force fighter that had escaped destruction during the Luftwaffe's earlier bombing of the frontier airfields. One such, an I-16 brought down mid-morning, provided the first victory for future Knight's Cross recipient Leutnant Walter Zellot.

But before the morning was out the first waves of bombers from the Soviet hinterland were being sent in against the invading German forces. Invariably unescorted, they fell easy prey to the waiting Messerschmitts. By day's end all but the first three of I./JG 53's 18 victories had taken the form of twin-engined bombers.

Meanwhile, Major von Maltzahn's *Geschwaderstab* had been flying a succession of *freie Jagd* and ground-attack sorties over the same areas to the north and east of Brest-Litovsk. The *Kommodore* himself got the first of the morning's trio of I-153 fighters, and then also claimed one of the three bombers downed in the afternoon.

Compared to the opening day's aerial activity, the Red Air Force was conspicuous by its absence throughout 23 June. Von Maltzahn and his

Despite the magnitude of the operation, there were still the odd moments of relaxation to be had at the start of *Barbarossa*. Here, enjoying the summer sun, are Hauptmann Franz von Werra (centre), *Gruppenkommandeur* of I./JG 53, and Leutnant Wolfgang Tonne. The machine in the background is Tonne's, its single chevron denoting his present position as *Gruppen-Adjutant*

With his arms crossed, Major von Maltzahn chats to two members of his *Geschwader Stabsschwarm* (section of four aircraft) at Dubno-South on 7 July 1941. The *Kommodore* and Leutnant Franz Schiess (second right) each claimed a Tupolev bomber on this day's early morning mission, but Leutnant Karl-Heinz Preu (right) returned not only empty-handed, but wounded in the left arm by return fire. His arm in a sling, he now awaits transport back to Germany for treatment

*Stabsschwarm* did not engage a single enemy aircraft, but concentrated instead on mounting further attacks on the Soviet ground columns that were already streaming eastwards away from the border regions.

I./JG 53 managed to bring down a single bomber on day two of the campaign. Credited to the *Kommandeur*, this was Oberleutnant Balfanz's first victory since taking command of the *Gruppe* – but it was also his last, for 24 hours later he was killed by return fire when attacking a clutch of Tupolev bombers to the northeast of Brest-Litovsk. Once again, Oberleutnant Ignaz Prestele, the *Kapitän* of 2. *Staffel*, stepped into the breach as acting-*Kommandeur* until the arrival of Balfanz's successor.

This was to be Hauptmann Franz von Werra, who, as a member of JG 3, had been shot down and captured over Kent at the height of the Battle of Britain. Since that time he had become something of a celebrity as the 'one that got away' by escaping while a PoW in Canada and successfully returning to Germany via a then still neutral USA.

Von Werra did not take over until 1 July 1941, by which time *Stab* and I./JG 53 had moved forward some 145 kilometres inside Soviet territory in the wake of *Panzergruppe* 2's advance on Bobruisk. In the process it had continued to protect the armoured spearheads from the attentions of the Red Air Force, claiming 30 bombers (and a brace of I-153 fighters) before the end of June.

Then, on 30 June, von Maltzahn's units were ordered to transfer from Baranovichi southwestwards to Hostynne, back in German-controlled Poland. This move took them across the army group boundary into the southern sector of the front. They were now operating under the control of *Luftflotte* 4, but

41

*General der Flieger* **Robert** *Ritter* **von Greim, GOC V.** *Fliegerkorps,* **visits JG 53's Tyranovka base in mid-July. While coffee is poured for the distinguished guest,** *Kommodore* **von Maltzahn (centre) briefs him on the current situation**

**Less than a fortnight later, and Major von Maltzahn finds himself in even more exalted company – and this time he is the visitor as he is summoned to the** *Führer's* **'Wolf's Lair' HQ in East Prussia to receive the Oak Leaves on 24 July from the hands of Adolf Hitler. Flanking von Maltzahn are Major Günther Lützow, the** *Kommodore* **of JG 3 (left) and Oberleutnant Josef 'Pips' Priller,** *Staffelkapitän* **of 1./JG 26 (right), both of whom were awarded their Oak Leaves on the same occasion**

their primary task remained the same – securing the skies above the advancing ground armour. The only differences were that the tanks skirting the southern edges of the Pripyet Marshes beneath them belonged to *Panzergruppe* 1, and their objective was not Bobruisk on the road to Moscow, but Kiev, the capital of the Ukraine.

This was to be the unit's main area of operations during its final five or six weeks' participation in *Barbarossa*. While at Hostynne things remained fairly quiet, but once it began leapfrogging forward into former Soviet territory to keep pace with the advancing Panzers, individual and collective scores started to climb dramatically.

Not surprisingly, perhaps, the lion's share of the *Geschwaderstab's* successes continued to go to the *Kommodore*. Major Günther *Freiherr* von Maltzahn had been awarded the Knight's Cross back in December 1940 for the then unusually low total of 13 enemy aircraft destroyed. The yardstick at the time was 20 kills, but perhaps von Maltzahn was also being honoured for his powers of leadership (and not, as some unkindly

suggested, as another snub to the recently departed – and still Knight's Cross-less – von Cramon-Taubadel).

Whatever the truth of the matter, 'Henri' von Maltzahn arrived on the eastern front with 15 kills under his belt. In less than a month he had added 24 more. And number 42 – a Pe-2 claimed on 24 July – earned him pride of place as the 'Ace of Spades'' first winner of the Oak Leaves.

By now *Stab* and I./JG 53 were based at Byelaya-Zirkov, 80 kilometres south of Kiev. This important communications centre had been occupied by the tanks of *Panzergruppe* 1 eight days earlier at the start of a gigantic armoured pincer movement aimed at encircling and capturing Kiev. But although they had been flying three or more missions daily in support of Army Group South's armoured divisions up to this point, von Maltzahn's pilots were not to witness the fall of the Ukrainian capital.

Early in August they were ordered to hand over their remaining serviceable *Friedrichs* to JG 3, with whom they were sharing Byelaya-Zirkov, and then entrain for their home base of Mannheim-Sandhofen, where they were to re-equip with brand new Bf 109F-4s.

During its first foray against the Soviet Union, I./JG 53 had been credited with more than 130 Red Air Force machines destroyed. It had cost the unit one pilot killed, two missing and one captured, plus several more wounded or injured.

After being withdrawn from the Channel coast on 8 June, II./JG 53 had likewise been deployed to the eastern front. But Hauptmann Heinz Bretnütz's *Gruppe* arrived in East Prussia only two *Staffeln* strong, 6./JG 53 having been detached from the parent unit to undertake defence duties along the Reich's North Sea coastline.

Based at Neusiedel, close to East Prussia's border with Lithuania, the truncated II. *Gruppe* was subordinated to JG 54 and formed part of *Luftflotte* 1 – the air fleet assigned to support ground operations on the northern sector of the front.

II./JG 53's part in *Barbarossa* began shortly before 0300 hrs on 22 June, when its pilots took off for an inconclusive *freie Jagd* sweep along the Lithuanian frontier region. Less than three hours later they were aloft again in response to reports of incoming Tupolev SB-2 bombers. The attackers were already retiring back into Lithuania by the time Bretnütz and his pilots caught up with them. It was to prove a fateful encounter.

Although six of the twin-engined Tupolevs were brought down in as many minutes, return fire from the fleeing formation severely damaged the *Kommandeur*'s machine. The wounded Bretnütz was forced to put down behind enemy lines. He was found and cared for by the local community until the arrival of the first German troops in the area four days later. By then, however, his wounds had turned gangrenous. And although he was immediately airlifted back to hospital, he died on 27 June. He was thus the second *Gruppenkommandeur* of JG 53 to be lost during the opening weeks of *Barbarossa* – both of them as a result of attacking Tupolev bombers.

Hauptmann Walter Spies, a member of the *Stabsschwarm*, had immediately taken over the *Gruppe*. His first victories of the war had been two of the six SB-2s downed during the recent engagement in which 'Pietsch' Bretnütz had been wounded.

By the evening of 22 June, 4. and 5./JG 53 had added five more Soviet bombers to the morning's half-dozen. And the seemingly ubiquitous

**Hauptmann Heinz Bretnütz, *Gruppenkommandeur* of II./JG 53, died as a result of wounds received on the opening day of Operation *Barbarossa***

Despite the loss of their *Kommandeur*, the morale of II. *Gruppe*'s pilots remained high. Here toasts are being drunk 'in the field' to their early successes against the Red Air Force. Among the pilots pictured is Feldwebel Josef Wurmheller (in swimming trunks, second from the right)

Tupolevs would continue to provide the main opposition as the two *Staffeln* began to stage northeastwards through the Baltic states of Lithuania and Latvia. At first they were employed primarily on uneventful *freie Jagd* patrols along the Baltic coastline (when not being scrambled in response to yet another Red Air Force bombing raid). Then, towards the end of June, by which time they were based at Kreuzberg, some 75 miles east of the Latvian capital Riga, they joined forces with elements of JG 54 in more direct support of the ground campaign.

In the northern sector this campaign was centred around *Panzergruppe* 4's rapid advance on Leningrad. As the leading armoured divisions raced across Estonia and smashed through the defences of the Stalin Line into the Soviet Union proper to the south of Lake Peipus, Hauptmann Spies' two *Staffeln* kept pace with them. During much of the first three weeks they not only protected the ground forces against attack from enemy bombers, but also flew escort missions for *Luftflotte* 1's own bomber and Stuka raids. These operations assured them of a steadily lengthening scoreboard, as many as nine or ten kills on some days.

The successes were evenly distributed throughout the two *Staffeln*, for since the loss of 32-victory Hauptmann Heinz Bretnütz, the *Gruppe* could boast of no single outstanding personality. Only four pilots, in fact, had as yet managed to raise their scores into double figures.

Still clad more for the beach than for *Barbarossa*, 'Sepp' Wurmheller poses alongside his 'Black 3'. The 18 victory markings date this picture as post-12 July 1941. Wurmheller would claim just one more kill with JG 53 – a Tupolev SB-2 on 15 July – before being transferred to III./JG 2 'Richthofen' in the west, where he would rise to prominence as one of the foremost *Experten* on the Channel front

Another inevitable result of all this activity was a corresponding decline in their serviceability figures. The units were operating at half strength or below when, on 19 July, they were ordered back into Estonia and thence to East Prussia for re-equipment with new Bf 109F-4s.

By the time 4. and 5./JG 53 returned to the eastern front in mid-August, German ground forces were already approaching the outer defences of Leningrad. Deployed on fields to the south of the city, it was this region – together with that along the River Volkhov flowing

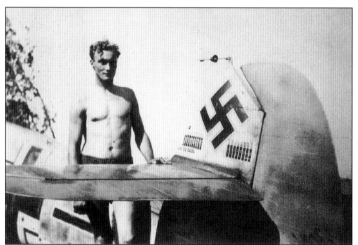

northwards into Lake Ladoga – that would be their main area of operations for the next seven weeks. The near-suicidal attacks by waves of largely unescorted twin-engined bombers that had marked the opening rounds of *Barbarossa* were now becoming a thing of the past, and it is a telling fact that of the 83 victories credited to II./JG 53 in the east during June and July, less than ten had been identified as fighters.

Instead, the Luftwaffe was beginning to encounter newer and more modern enemy bomber types – pilots of 5./JG 53 claimed their first trio of Il-2 *Sturmoviks* on 8 September – while the portly Polikarpov fighters of pre-war vintage were slowly giving way to less antiquated in-line-engined machines. But the *Staffeln's* Bf 109F-4s proved more than a match for these newcomers, pilots in their Messerschmitt fighters continuing to inflict losses on the Red Air Force – again, sometimes ten a day in August and September – at minimal cost to themselves.

During its time on the Leningrad front, II./JG 53 lost three pilots – one in a dogfight, one to anti-aircraft fire and the third in a take-off accident. A fourth was seriously wounded. Oberfeldwebel Stefan Litjens of 4. *Staffel* had already claimed two victories on 11 September – taking his overall score to 23 – when, during the course of a Stuka escort mission, his *Friedrich* was hit by Russian fighters. Although he managed to bail out over friendly territory and was immediately rushed to a hospital in Riga, surgeons were unable to save the sight of his right eye.

Two other pilots saw their scores pass the 20 mark while on the northern sector – *Gruppen-Adjutant* Oberleutnant Gerhard Michalski, who reached 22, and the *Kapitän* of 5. *Staffel*, Oberleutnant Kurt Brändle, who got 29. Just one year earlier, a total of 20 enemy aircraft destroyed was an almost cast-iron guarantee of a Knight's Cross, but the staggering number of kills racked up by many Luftwaffe fighter pilots during the first three months of *Barbarossa* had rendered this arbitrary yardstick meaningless.

**Oberfeldwebel Stefan Litjens' scoreboard traces his career to date – two victories against the French, five over the RAF and 15 in Russia. The last shown here was for a Tupolev bomber downed on the morning of 11 September. 'Steff' Litjens (right) is now waiting to go up again. This same afternoon he will add number 23 – an 'I-18' fighter – but the day's third mission will end with his being shot down by an I-16 and result in the loss of his right eye**

And so, when the members of II./JG 53 were recalled from Russia for the second and final time on 6 October 1941, there was not one Knight's Cross wearer among them.

It was to be a different story entirely for III./JG 53. When Hauptmann Wolf-Dietrich Wilcke's *Gruppe* departed Wiesbaden-Erbenheim on 12 June 1941, it too was destined for the central sector of the eastern front. Unlike the *Geschwaderstab* and I./JG 53, however, it was to operate on the extreme left-hand flank of Army Group Centre, close to the boundary with Army Group North. For this purpose the *Gruppe* was based at Sobolevo – formerly in northern Poland, but now incorporated into East Prussia – alongside II./JG 52, both *Gruppen* being subordinated to JG 27 for the launch of *Barbarossa*.

It was 0320 hrs on 22 June when Hauptmann Wilcke's pilots took off on the first of an almost 18-hour-long series of low-level attacks on Soviet frontier airfields. Interspersed with several Stuka escort missions, these were so successful that by day's end III./JG 53 had been credited with a staggering 36 Soviet aircraft shot down – the highest number of any *Jagdgruppe* involved on the opening day of the campaign in the east – plus a further 28 destroyed on the ground. The aerial victories included five for *'Fürst'* Wilcke and four for 9. *Staffel's* Leutnant Erich Schmidt, taking their totals to 18 and 21 respectively. It had cost the *Gruppe* just two Bf 109s written off in forced landings.

Although employed on similar operations for the next two days, III./JG 53's pilots encountered little opposition in the air and did not claim a single victory. It was not until 25 June, when the *Gruppe* moved forward to Vilnius, in Lithuania, captured just 24 hours earlier, that the Red Air Force reappeared in any strength. By this time, in addition to its ground attack and bomber escort duties, the *Gruppe* was also flying cover for the leading armoured divisions of *Panzergruppe* 3 as they began to advance on Minsk, the capital of White Russia.

In the three days leading up to 27 June (the date the encirclement of Minsk was completed), III./JG 53 added 56 Soviet aircraft to its combined total. Seven of these had fallen to Erich Schmidt, who thus continued to maintain his position as the *Gruppe's* highest scorer.

Surrounded first from the north by *Panzergruppe* 3 and then from the south by *Panzergruppe* 2, Minsk developed into one of the first great 'cauldron' battles of the Russian front. By its close on 9 July, the German army had taken nearly a third of a million Soviet prisoners and destroyed or captured more than 3000 Russian tanks.

During the initial stages of the battle the *Gruppe* patrolled to the north and east of the white Russian capital. Its main task was to protect the ground troops from the Soviet bombers attempting to blast open an escape route for the trapped Red Army units. To increase its fighting strength, III./JG 53 temporarily joined forces with II./JG 52 on 1 July to form the *Gefechtsverband* 'Wilcke'. In the first three days of its existence this *ad hoc* combat command accounted for no fewer than 36 Ilyushin DB-3 bombers, plus a dozen fighters and other types.

On 4 July Leutnant Erich Schmidt of 9./JG 53 downed an I-16 fighter. This was his 30th victory of the war, and would earn him the Knight's Cross 19 days later. It was only the second such decoration for the *Gruppe* since Werner Mölders had won the first back in May 1940.

As *Barbarossa* gathered momentum and pilots' individual scores began to climb, III./JG 53 also played host to a number of senior officers. One such visitor was Generaloberst Wolfram *Freiherr* von Richthofen, GOC VIII. *Fliegerkorps*, who is seen here chatting to Leutnant Erich Schmidt after presenting him with the Knight's Cross on 23 July 1941. While von Richthofen presumably dropped in by *Storch* (note the tail of the Fi 156 in the background) . . .

Leaving follow-up units of Army Group Centre to carry out the final reduction of the Minsk cauldron, the spearheads of *Panzergruppe* 3 continued their advance eastwards. They took Vitebsk on 9 July and then wheeled down towards Smolensk, their next objective on the road to Moscow. Only some 230 miles from the Soviet capital, Smolensk was to fall to elements of *Panzergruppe* 2 driving up from the south on 16 July.

III./JG 53 leapfrogged forward, keeping pace with the rampaging armour – firstly to Lepel, southwest of Vitebsk, on 6 July, which was yet another field wrested only hours earlier from the enemy – before then staging onwards to arrive at Mozhna, northeast of Smolensk, by month's end. Soviet resistance in the air to this sustained onslaught increased steadily during the latter half of July 1941. So, too, did the length of the *Gruppe's* scoreboard, with more than three-dozen victories on 26 and 27 July alone – all but four of them were twin-engined bombers.

Then, on 2 August, III./JG 53 parted company with *Stab* JG 27. While the latter (together with the still attached II./JG 52) was transferred northwards to the Leningrad front, Hauptmann Wilcke's *Gruppe* remained on the central sector, where it now formed part of the *Gefechtsverband* 'Hagen'. This was a Ju 87 Stuka strike force named after its leader, Major Walter Hagen, *Geschwaderkommodore* of StG 1, especially created to support 9. *Armée's* forthcoming attack on the town of Velikiye Luki – a Soviet stronghold astride the northern approach to Moscow.

Three days before his unit joined Hagen's command, Hauptmann Dietrich Wilcke had claimed his 25th kill. And three days after joining the *Gefechtsverband*, the second of a pair of Pe-2s credited to 8./JG 53's Leutnant Herbert Schramm took his total to the quarter-century too. This resulted in both men being awarded the Knight's Cross on 6 August.

**. . . Generalfeldmarschall Albert Kesselring arrived at Surash on 9 August in his personally-badged Fw 189 to present the Knight's Crosses, announced three days earlier, to Leutnant Herbert Schramm (left) and Hauptmann Wolf-Dietrich Wilcke (second right). Erich Schmidt joins them for a souvenir photo, which also offers a clue as to why Kesselring was popularly known as 'Smiling Albert'!**

Although III./JG 53 was to spend much of August in direct support of the fighting around Velikiye Luki, its contribution was not all it might have been. The level of operations over the past six weeks had seriously reduced its strength, and this, coupled with an almost complete breakdown in the supply of spares, meant that by the middle of the month the *Gruppe* did not have a single machine serviceable.

The situation slowly began to improve, however, and in the last week of August – despite still being at less than half strength – Wilcke's pilots managed to bring down more than 50 aircraft. On the last day of the month, their successes included all six of a formation of bombers that were destroyed by a *Schwarm* from 9./JG 53 led by future Knight's Cross recipient Oberleutnant Franz Götz (whose own kill on this occasion raised his personal tally to 25). But this event was overshadowed on that same 31 August by the loss of 9. *Staffel*'s Erich Schmidt. He had taken off for a *freie Jagd* of the area to the east of Velikiye Luki accompanied by his wingman, Oberleutnant Josef Kronschnabel. The latter takes up the story;

'As we could find no enemy in the air, we went down to strafe some machines on a Russian airfield. While we were doing so, Schmidt's aircraft was hit by ground fire and burst into flames. He managed to pull it up, turn it over on to its back and bail out.'

Kronschnabel saw Leutnant Schmidt land safely not far from the airfield they had just been attacking, but all trace of him disappeared after that. With 47 victories to his credit, '*Schmidtchen*' ('Little Smithy') was still the *Gruppe*'s top scorer at the time he was reported missing.

Less than a week after the loss of Erich Schmidt, III./JG 53 was on the move again. On 5 September it was ordered to cross the army group boundary and fly down to Ossiyaki, in the southern sector. No longer part of the *Gefechtsverband* 'Hagen', it was now subordinated to V. *Fliegerkorps*. Although this corps was mainly a mixed bomber force, the *Gruppe* was initially employed on *freie Jagd* sweeps in support of the armoured spearheads of *Panzergruppe* 1 as they drove southeastwards towards Kiev.

This would remain III./JG 53's area of operations throughout September, for while the city itself was to fall on the 19th, another massive cauldron battle developed to the east of the Ukrainian capital. Here the fighting raged for a further seven days, finally ending on 26 September with the capture of an estimated 665,000 Red Army troops.

Hauptmann Wilcke's pilots were heavily involved in the Kiev operations. Abandoning their earlier *freie Jagd* role, they now began to fly

III./JG 53's sole casualty of 31 August was recent Knight's Cross recipient Leutnant Erich Schmidt of 9. *Staffel*. His 'Yellow 6' was hit by Soviet anti-aircraft fire and the *Gruppe*'s top scorer took to his parachute over enemy territory, only then to disappear without trace

8. *Staffel*'s Oberfeldwebel Adolf Kalkum was more fortunate six days later when he was able to put his 'Black 4' down on its belly in what appears to be a field of clover near III. *Gruppe*'s base to the north of Kiev. The figure in the light flying blouse among the group inspecting the damage is Herbert Schramm

escort missions for the bomber and Stuka units attacking tank and troop concentrations within the cauldron, as well as mounting ground-attack sorties of their own against Red Army truck convoys and troop columns.

In addition to their considerable ground successes, this netted them a steady toll of aerial opponents. Although not on a scale to compare with the opening days and weeks of *Barbarossa*, they nonetheless claimed a creditable 60 kills during the three weeks of the fighting around Kiev.

On 14 September, as if making up for lost time, the *Gruppe* won its fourth Knight's Cross in the space of less than two weeks. The recipient was the *Stabsschwarm*'s Oberleutnant Friedrich-Karl Müller. But quite how, or why, he in particular was selected for the honour is no longer clear. His score at the time was standing at exactly 20 – a benchmark figure long since overtaken by events. And there were at least five other members of the *Gruppe* whose current totals exceeded Müller's – some by as many as eight victories. Of these five, three would amass 40 kills and have to wait up to twelve months before receiving their Knight's Crosses, and the remaining two were each awarded the German Cross in Gold in early 1942.

III./JG 53's final move in Russia took it to Konotop on 16 September. It was from here, little more than 30 miles from the northeastern rim of the Kiev cauldron, that the unit would claim the last 20 or so of its nearly 375 victories against the Red Air Force – achieved at a cost of just four pilots killed, missing or captured – before being ordered to return to the Reich on 4 October 1941.

Throughout its 16-week participation in the opening stages of the campaign in the east, JG 53 had also maintained a presence in the embryonic defence of the Reich organisation.

At first, this presence consisted solely of 6./JG 53, which had been detached from its parent II. *Gruppenstab* five days before the latter departed France for Mannheim-Sandhofen on 8 June 1941. Thus, while the bulk of II./JG 53 began preparations for its move to the eastern front, Oberleutnant Otto Böhner's 6. *Staffel* was already settling in at Jever, close to Germany's North Sea coast. Here, subordinated to *Stab* JG 1, its task was to be the aerial defence of the German Bight.

In the summer of 1941, however, this area was something of an operational backwater during the hours of daylight (although RAF Bomber Command had long been attacking the ports along Germany's northern seaboard under cover of darkness). Perhaps as a result of this dearth of activity, 6./JG 53 was transferred to Döberitz, close to Berlin, during the third week in June, only to return to the North Sea sector early the following month. It now took up residence at Westerland, on the island of Sylt, where it would remain until late August.

With 6./JG 53 safely ensconced on Sylt, and with the pilots having little more to do than familiarise themselves with their new Bf 109F-4s, now would perhaps be a convenient time to break off the narrative and chronicle the brief, but complex, history of another component of JG 53 currently based in the west.

## ERGANZUNGSSTAFFEL

Early in the war it had become the practice for each *Jagdgeschwader* to form its own *Ergänzungsstaffel*, or 'replacement squadron'. These were, in effect, quasi-operational training units to which newly qualified fighter pilots were sent to acquire practical experience prior to an operational posting to one of the *Geschwader*'s frontline *Gruppen*. Although an integral part of the *Geschwader* for administrative purposes, the *Ergänzungsstaffel* was often geographically far removed from its *Stab*, usually in some quiet corner of occupied western Europe.

JG 53's *Ergänzungsstaffel* was one of the first to be established. Commanded by Hauptmann Hubert Kroeck (ex-*Staffelkapitän* of 4./JG 53), it had been activated at Fontenet, in France, towards the end of September 1940. Two months later a *Gruppenstab* and another *Staffel* were formed. The latter, somewhat confusingly, was then designated 1.(*Einsatz*) – i.e. operational – *Ergänzungsstaffel* JG 53, while the original unit became 2. (*Schul*) *Ergänzungsstaffel* JG 53.

The procedure was now for pilots to serve with 2. (*Schul*) – school – *Staffel*, before then progressing to 1. *Staffel* to gain operational experience. In order to be able to provide such experience, 1. *Einsatzstaffel* occupied a succession of fields along the French Channel and Biscay seaboards for much of 1941, while 2. *Staffel* remained for the most part further removed from the scene of any possible enemy activity.

It was on 16 February that the *Ergänzungsgruppe* claimed its first victory – a Blenheim bomber reportedly shot down into the Channel off the mouth of the River Somme (although RAF records fail to corroborate this). More than five months were to pass before the *Gruppe* achieved its next, far more emphatic, and final successes against RAF Bomber Command.

The British had for some time been planning a major daylight bombing raid – involving some 150 aircraft in all – against the German battlecruisers *Scharnhorst* and *Gneisenau*, which were holed up in Brest harbour. At the last minute, however, it was discovered that the *Scharnhorst* had departed Brest for La Pallice, more than 150 miles further to the south along the Biscay coast. The attack, carried out on 24 July, had therefore to be split in two. While nearly 100 twin-engined bombers were despatched against the *Gneisenau* in Brest, a force of 15 Halifax heavy bombers made the longer haul down to La Pallice. Here, they were confronted by the Bf 109Es of 2. *Schulstaffel*, scrambled from nearby La Rochelle and led by the unit's more experienced NCO instructors.

In a running fight lasting more than half-an-hour, the *Staffel* claimed the destruction of six Halifaxes (in fact, five were lost, and all the remainder damaged) at the cost to themselves of just one *Emil*, whose pilot bailed out to safety.

During the latter half of October 1941, the *Ergänzungsgruppe* was withdrawn from France back into the Reich. For the next three months the two *Staffeln* continued their training activities out of Düsseldorf-Lohausen. The *Gruppe*'s end came with the wholesale restructuring of the training organisation early in 1942. Only 2. *Schulstaffel* would remain in the training role, being incorporated into the newly formed *Ergänzungsjagdgruppe* South (where it continued to turn out pilots destined for frontline service with JG 53). More immediate practical use was made of the operational expertise already gained by the *Gruppenstab* and 1. *Einsatzstaffel* when these were redesignated to become *Stab* IV./JG 1 and 1./JG 3 respectively.

Meanwhile, what of Oberleutnant Böhner's 6./JG 53, last heard of in splendid isolation up on the German North Sea island of Sylt? Its tranquil idyll had been rudely terminated on 21 August 1941 when the *Staffel* was

The wreckage of the No 257 Sqn Hurricane that provided 6./JG 53's Leutnant Helmut Rose with his first victory on 15 September 1941. It was still lying close to the crash site near Bergen aan Zee airfield two months later when this photograph was taken. The RAF fighter was Rose's sole victory while with JG 53

ordered down to Katwijk, on the Dutch coast. This brought it within effective range of the RAF, whose 'lean into France' of the early summer months was slowly being extended eastwards into the Low Countries.

Exactly one week after its arrival at Katwijk, 6./JG 53 engaged a low-level raid by Blenheims on shipping in Rotterdam docks. Leutnant Hans Möller was credited with two of the seven bombers brought down in the target area. The *Staffel* also claimed two of the bombers' escorting Spitfires.

On 4 September 6./JG 53 made the short hop northwards along the Dutch coast from Katwijk to Bergen aan Zee. And before the month was out the *Staffel* had added two more RAF machines to its collective total – a Hurricane on 15 September and a Wellington two weeks later.

It was at this juncture that 6. *Staffel* was joined in the Netherlands by the first returnees from Russia. Both the *Geschwaderstab* and I./JG 53 had been withdrawn from the eastern front during the first week of August. Having converted onto F-4s at Mannheim-Sandhofen in the interim, they were now ordered forward to Katwijk (with 2. *Staffel* being deployed first to Haastede and then to Flushing to guard the Maas and Scheldt Estuaries).

Early October also saw the arrival of *Stab*, 4. and 5./JG 53, who had staged almost directly from the Leningrad front with only a 48-hour stopover at Insterburg, in East Prussia, *en route*. Instead of rejoining 6. *Staffel* at Bergen aan Zee immediately, however, they would spend their first month at Leeuwarden, in northern Holland.

October's five kills would be shared between I. and II. *Gruppen*. The experienced 6./JG 53 claimed the first – a Whitley returning from a night raid on Essen, shot down off the Dutch coast shortly after first light on 11th. Then it was 4. *Staffel*'s turn. It was credited with a brace of Blenheims caught while attacking a coastal convoy off the island of Texel on 27 October.

In the meantime, I. *Gruppe* had also accounted for an anti-shipping Blenheim, downed off Katwijk on 21 October, plus a Spitfire (possibly only damaged) three days later.

But on 25 October I./JG 53 was dealt a double blow, not only suffer-ing the *Geschwader*'s only known combat fatality of its time in Holland,

Hauptmann Franz von Werra, *Gruppenkommandeur* of I./JG 53, whose *Friedrich* crashed into the North Sea off Katwijk on 25 October 1941

when a pilot of 2. *Staffel* was killed in action against Spitfires near Flushing, but also losing its *Kommandeur*, Hauptmann Franz von Werra. The latter's *Friedrich* was seen to nose-dive into the sea off Katwijk, presumably as a result of engine failure. An eye-witness reported that von Werra's machine – without any prior warning, and with no signs of fire or other damage – suddenly tipped forward onto its nose and almost immediately hit the surface of the sea.

Another Knight's Cross wearer, Hauptmann Herbert Kaminski, an ex-*Zerstörer* pilot latterly serving on the staff of the *General der Jagdflieger*, arrived at Katwijk on 1 November to replace the fallen von Werra.

It was also early in November that the last of JG 53's three component *Gruppen* reappeared on the Luftwaffe's western front order of battle. Having been withdrawn from the Kiev area on 4 October, III./JG 53 had likewise utilised the intervening time at Mannheim-Sandhofen to re-equip with a full complement of F-4s. It then transferred up to Husum, in Schleswig-Holstein, on 8 November to serve under *Stab* JG 1.

But the *Gruppe's* sojourn in Germany's northernmost province was to be brief in the extreme. After only six days it was recalled to Mannheim to make hurried preparations for another move. Having been the last *Gruppe* to return to the west from Russia, III./JG 53 was now about to become the first to depart for the *Geschwader's* next major theatre of operations – the Mediterranean.

Mindful of the growing threat of RAF bombing raids, II./JG 53 went to great lengths to disguise its hangars and other buildings at Bergen aan Zee. This 'windmill' sits atop the *Gruppe's* camouflaged workshop!

# COLOUR PLATES

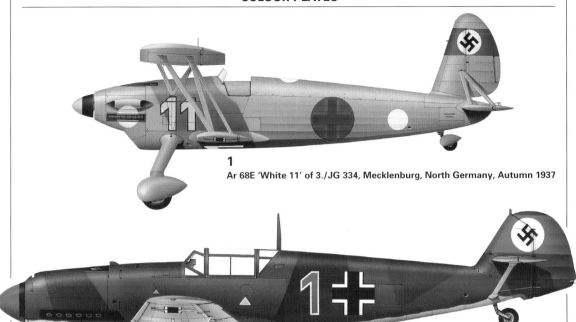

**1**
Ar 68E 'White 11' of 3./JG 334, Mecklenburg, North Germany, Autumn 1937

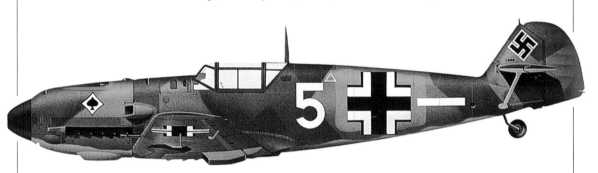

**2**
Bf 109D-1 'Red 1' of Oberleutnant Rolf Pingel, *Staffelkapitän* 2./JG 334, Wiesbaden-Erbenheim, October 1938

**3**
Bf 109E 'White 5' of Unteroffizier Stefan Litjens, 4./JG 53, Mannheim-Sandhofen, October 1939

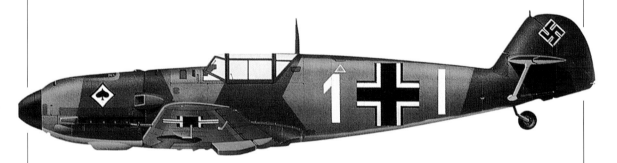

**4**
Bf 109E 'White 1' of Oberleutnant Wolf-Dietrich Wilcke, *Staffelkapitän* 7./JG 53, Wiesbaden-Erbenheim, October 1939

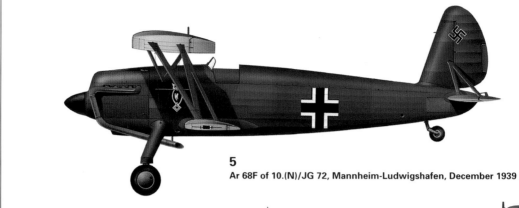

**5**
Ar 68F of 10.(N)/JG 72, Mannheim-Ludwigshafen, December 1939

**6**
Bf 109E 'Black Chevron-Triangle' of Hauptmann Werner Mölders, *Gruppenkommandeur* III./JG 53, Trier-Euren, March 1940

**7**
Bf 109E 'Red 5' of Feldwebel Hans Kornatz, 2./JG 53, Darmstadt-Griesheim, April 1940

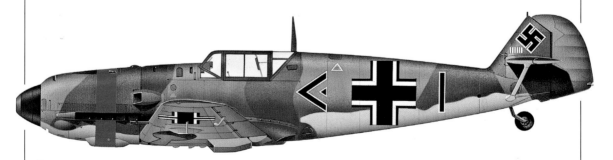

**8**
Bf 109E 'Black Chevron-Triangle' of Hauptmann Harro Harder, *Gruppenkommandeur* III./JG 53, Villiaze/Guernsey, August 1940

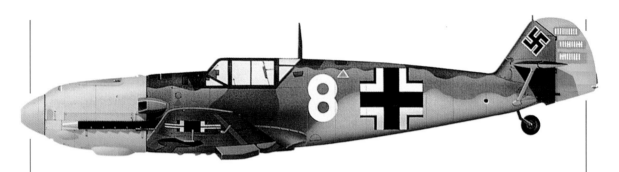

**9**
Bf 109E 'White 8' of Hauptmann Hans-Karl Mayer, *Gruppenkommandeur* I./JG 53, Etaples, September 1940

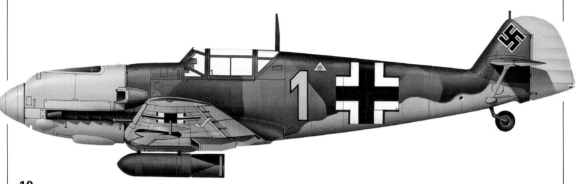

**10**
Bf 109E 'Yellow 1' of Oberleutnant Walter Rupp, *Staffelkapitän* 3./JG 53, Le Touquet, October 1940

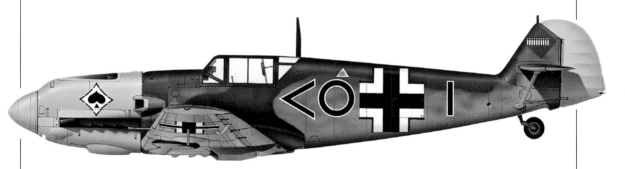

**11**
Bf 109E 'Black Chevron Circle' of Oberleutnant Friedrich Karl Müller, *Gruppen-TO* III./JG 53, Le Touquet, November 1940

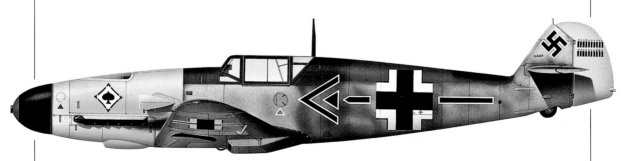

**12**
Bf 109F-2 'Black Chevron-Triangle and Bars' of Major Günther *Freiherr* von Maltzahn, *Geschwaderkommodore* JG 53, St Omer-Wizernes, May 1941

**13**
Bf 109F-2 'Black Chevron-Triangle' of Hauptmann Heinz Bretnütz, *Gruppenkommandeur* II./JG 53, St Omer-Clairmarais,
May 1941

**14**
Bf 109F-2 'Black Chevron-Triangle' of Hauptmann Wolf-Dietrich Wilcke, *Gruppenkommandeur* III./JG 53, Maldeghem,
June 1941

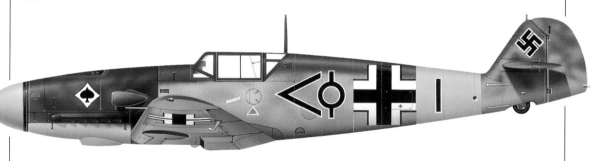

**15**
Bf 109F-2 'Black Chevron and Circle/Bar' of Leutnant Jürgen Harder, *Gruppenstab* III./JG 53, Suwalki, June 1941

**16**
Bf 109F-2 'Black Chevron-Triangle and Bars' of Major Günther *Freiherr* von Maltzahn, *Geschwaderkommodore* JG 53,
Byelaya-Zirkov, July 1941

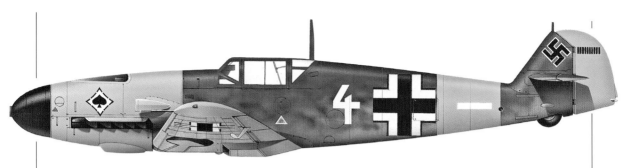

**17**
Bf 109F-4 'White 4' of Leutnant Fritz Dinger, 4./JG 53, Lyuban, October 1941

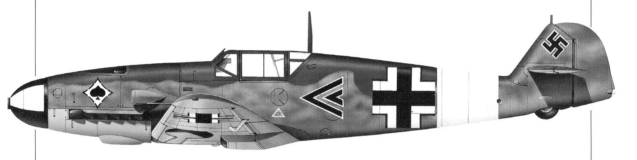

**18**
Bf 109F-4 'Black Double Chevron' of Hauptmann Herbert Kaminski, *Gruppenkommandeur* I./JG 53, San Pietro/Sicily, January 1942

**19**
Bf 109F 4/Z 'White 1' of Oberleutnant Werner Langemann, *Staffelkapitän* 10.(*Jabo*)/JG 53, San Pietro/Sicily, January 1942

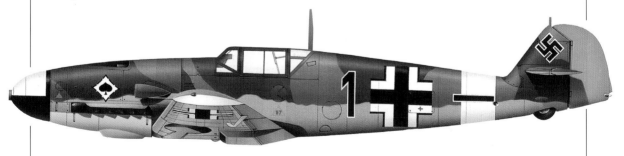

**20**
Bf 109F-4 'Black 1' of Hauptmann Kurt Brändle, *Staffelkapitän* 5./JG 53, Comiso/Sicily, April 1942

**21**
Bf 109F-4/trop 'White 5' of Leutnant Jürgen Harder, 7./JG 53, Martuba/Libya, June 1942

**22**
Bf 109F-4/trop 'Black Double Chevron' of Major Erich Gerlitz, *Gruppenkommandeur* III./JG 53, Quotaifiya, July 1942

**23**
Bf 109G-2 'Black 12' of Leutnant Walter Zellot, *Staffelkapitän* 2./JG 53, Tusov/Stalingrad Front, August 1942

**24**
Bf 109G-4/trop 'Black 1' of Oberleutnant Franz Schiess, *Staffelkapitän* 8./JG 53, Trapani/Sicily, February 1943

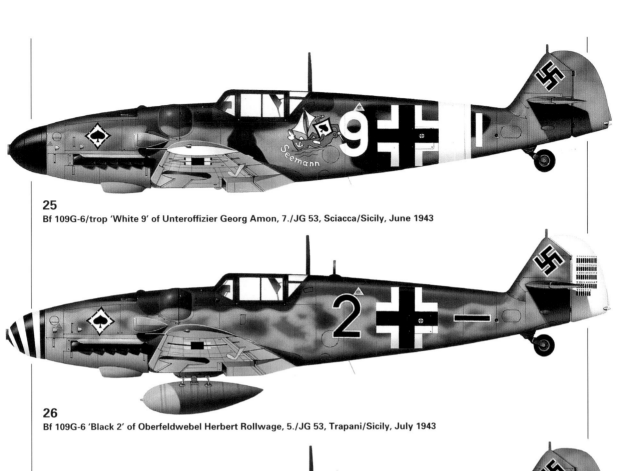

**25**
Bf 109G-6/trop 'White 9' of Unteroffizier Georg Amon, 7./JG 53, Sciacca/Sicily, June 1943

**26**
Bf 109G-6 'Black 2' of Oberfeldwebel Herbert Rollwage, 5./JG 53, Trapani/Sicily, July 1943

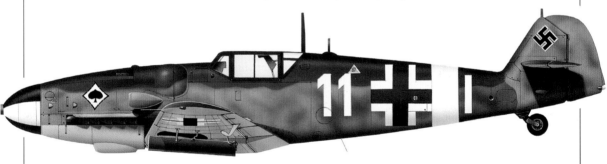

**27**
Bf 109G-6 'White 11' of 7./JG 53, Villa Orba/Italy, December 1943

**28**
Bf 109G-6 'Black 2' of Unteroffizier Otto Zendler, 8./JG 53, Villa Orba/Italy, December 1944

**29**
Bf 109G-6 'Black 2' of Oberfeldwebel Herbert Rollwage, 5./JG 53, Vienna-Seyring, January 1944

**30**
Bf 106G-6 'Yellow 1' of Leutnant Alfred Hammer, *Staffelkapitän* 6./JG 53, Vienna-Seyring, February 1944

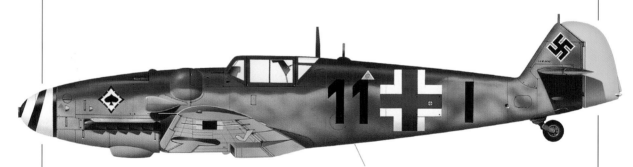

**31**
Bf 109G-6 'Black 11' of Unteroffizier Heinz Girnth, 8./JG 53, Bad Lippspringe, July 1944

**32**
Bf 109G-14/AS 'White 5' of Gefreiter Gerhard Michaelis, 7./JG 53, Hustedt, August 1944

**33**
Bf 109G-14 'Yellow 9' of 9./JG 53, Neuhausen ob Eck, December 1944

**34**
Bf 109K-4 'Yellow 1' of Leutnant Günther Landt, *Staffelkapitän* 11./JG 53, Kirrlach, February 1945

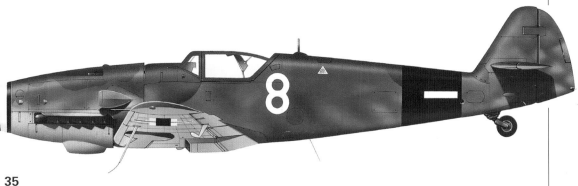

**35**
Bf 109G-14/AS 'White 8' of 7./JG 53, Malmsheim, March 1945

## UNIT HERALDRY

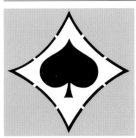

**1**
JG 53
worn on cowling of Bf 109E/F/G

**2**
10.(N)/JG 72
worn beneath windscreen of Ar 68E/F

**3**
10.(*Jabo*)/JG 53
worn on aft fuselage of Bf 109F

# THE MEDITERRANEAN, ACT I

**M**alta has been described as the 'hub of the Mediterranean'. Situated just 60 miles south of Sicily, not only is it on the main east-west Alexandria to Gibraltar shipping lane, it also sits directly astride the north to south supply route from Italy to Tripoli, the seaport capital of the then Italian colony of Libya. The island's geographical location thus had a profound effect on the Axis forces' ability to wage war in North Africa.

Heavily dependent upon seaborne supplies for their desert operations, the Italians and Germans had already tried to bomb Malta into submission – or at least inactivity – but without success. However parlous their own position became, British forces on the island continued to harry Axis supply vessels from both sea and air. Now the Luftwaffe was planning to launch a new offensive, and the unit earmarked to provide the main fighter protection for the bombers of II. *Fliegerkorps* was Major Günther von Maltzahn's JG 53.

The first part of the *Geschwader* to arrive in Sicily was III. *Gruppe*, who flew in to Catania on 3 December 1941. But on the far side of the Mediterranean by that date, Operation *Crusader* (Britain's second great Western Desert offensive) had already been underway for a fortnight. General Rommel's *Afrika Korps* was under severe pressure and, although not yet in full retreat, it desperately needed help.

Consequently, just three days after its arrival in Catania, III./JG 53 was on the move again, staging via a circuitous route through Italy, Greece and

An early casualty of III./JG 53's war in North Africa, Bf 109F-4/trop 'Yellow 5' of 9. *Staffel* has come to grief somewhere in the Libyan desert. An engineering officer has flown out in a *Storch* to assess the situation, and the possibilities of recovery

Crete, to Tmimi, in Libya, where it touched down on 8 December. Almost immediately, 8. *Staffel* was detached to Benina, 155 miles to the west, to defend the supply port of Benghazi. Given their abrupt departure from Sicily, there had been no time to train the *Gruppe*'s pilots for the rigours of desert operations, or to tropicalise the Bf 109Fs in any way.

Nor was their situation improved when two Ju 52/3m transports, bringing in members of the ground staff and technical equipment from Crete, were shot down by an over-enthusiastic – some say berserk – Italian fighter pilot as they approached to land at Tmimi!

Nevertheless, on only their second day in action – while escorting a formation of Ju 88s attacking Bir Hacheim – they were able to claim four Hurricanes without loss, the first being credited to *Gruppenkommandeur* Hauptmann Wolf-Dietrich Wilcke, taking his overall total to 35. But on the evening of that same 11 December, III./JG 53 was forced to evacuate Tmimi as the ground fighting drew closer. It had to blow up three of its unserviceable machines before leaving, and these – added to the four already written off by enemy bombing and in landing accidents at Tmimi – represented the loss of over a third of its effective strength.

Having pulled back from Tmimi to nearby Derna-West, the *Gruppe* flew a series of *freie Jagd* sweeps on 12 December, downing half-a-dozen Hurricanes and a single Tomahawk during the mid-afternoon mission – again without loss. It was on the following day, with the action centred above the hotly contested Gazala line, that III./JG 53 suffered its first combat casualty when a 7. *Staffel* pilot was shot down by a P-40 and suffered severe burns.

13 December had netted the *Gruppe* just two victories. Twenty-four hours later it would claim three – also over the Gazala battlefield – but at an even greater cost, with two more members of 7./JG 53 falling victim to P-40s. This time one was killed and the other reported missing.

Nor were 7./JG 53's misfortunes over yet. On 16 December the *Gruppe* was ordered to fly a number of reconnaissance missions down into the desert to try to locate the British armoured units that were attempting to outflank and cut off Rommel's forces now retreating along the coastal plain. The first to take off were Oberleutnant Heinz Altendorf, the *Kapitän* of 7. *Staffel*, and his wingman. They found the enemy tanks near Mechili, only for both to be brought down by anti-aircraft fire. And while Gefreiter Hartmut Klötzer managed to evade and make his way back to German-held territory on foot (only to be reported missing over Tunisia almost exactly a year later), the 24-victory Heinz Altendorf was destined to sit out the rest of the war in captivity.

The next day the *Gruppe*, having handed over its surviving machines to JG 27, was airlifted back to Sicily. Only the detached 8. *Staffel*, some 135 miles to the west at Benina, was still on African soil. It would remain here for a further five days, which was just long enough for the *Staffel* to suffer its only casualty – an NCO pilot wounded by return fire from South African Maryland bombers raiding Benghazi – before it too passed its *Friedrichs* over to JG 27 prior to being flown out of Libya. The 'Ace of Spades'' first brief expedition to Africa was at an end. But the *Geschwader* would be back six months hence.

By the time the members of III./JG 53 returned to Sicily in late December 1941, the rest of the *Geschwader* had already arrived. Major von Maltzahn's *Stab* and II. *Gruppe* were occupying Comiso, in the southeastern corner of the island, with I. *Gruppe* just over 20 miles away on the coast at Gela. For a number of reasons, not least the adverse weather and heavy rain at the turn of the year, the planned air assault on Malta had not yet begun in earnest. But JG 53's fighters were put to use virtually from the moment they arrived in Sivily.

The first to see action were the four aircraft of the *Geschwader's Stabsschwarm* (HQ flight), which were despatched on a *freie Jagd* sweep over Malta on 19 December, just four days after flying into Comiso. Despite the very bad weather in the target area, they encountered several Hurricanes, one of which was claimed by the *Kommodore* for his half-century. For the remainder of the month, which was marked by further squally rain and at times gale-force winds, the *Stab* continued to mount independent *freie Jagd* sorties against Malta. These resulted in five more victories (all Hurricanes), three of which also fell to Major von Maltzahn.

Unlike the *Stab's* purely free-ranging fighter patrols, I. and II. *Gruppen's* early operations against Malta also included their having to provide cover for small formations of Ju 88 bombers. The first such mission, flown by I./JG 53 on the morning of 20 December, consisted of 11 of the *Gruppe's Friedrichs* escorting four Ju 88s sent to attack shipping in the Grand Harbour of Valetta, the capital of Malta. They were intercepted by a dozen Hurricanes. In the confused melée that followed (there were other aircraft – German and Italian – over the Grand Harbour at the time), I./JG 53 claimed three of the British fighters without loss. *Gruppenkommandeur* Hauptmann Herbert Kaminski and Oberleutnant Friedrich-Karl Müller, the *Kapitän* of 1. *Staffel*, were each credited with one apiece.

II./JG 53's operational debut over Malta, on 23 December, was a similar mission involving the escort of Ju 88s – just two bombers this time – to Valetta. This raid was also intercepted by Hurricanes, one of the defenders being claimed off the Maltese coast (RAF records make no mention of such a loss, but do admit to two of its fighters having to force-land after suffering combat damage). The following day another Hurricane provided victory number 30 for Oberleutnant Kurt Brändle, the *Staffelkapitän* of 5./JG 53.

By year-end the *Geschwader* had been credited with exactly 20 Hurricanes destroyed, plus a single Blenheim caught while on patrol over open water. Its own combat casualties totalled just two pilots wounded.

The adverse weather conditions continued throughout much of January 1942, resulting in a marked decline in JG 53's operations against Malta. Only Hauptmann Walter Spies' II. *Gruppe* managed to add slowly to its collective scoreboard during this period, supplementing a steady diet of Hurricanes – 13 in all by the end of the month – with one or two less familiar types.

The unit's first successes of the New Year were a brace of Hurricanes claimed during a Ju 88 escort mission to bomb Luqa airfield on 3 January. But this raid also resulted in the *Geschwader's* first loss over Malta when a 4. *Staffel* machine exploded in mid-air after being hit by anti-aircraft fire. A second attack on Luqa 24 hours later gave rise to claims for four more Hurricanes. But then nine days were to pass before II./JG 53 was credited with its next victim – another Blenheim shot down into the Mediterranean.

Snug in its dispersal pen at Comiso, 6. *Staffel*'s 'Yellow 12' casts a strong noonday shadow, proving that Sicily enjoyed *some* sunshine in the opening weeks of 1942. This machine may be the F-4/Z that five-victory Leutnant Herbert Soukup bailed out of over Malta on 15 May when its port wing was blown off by cannon fire from a No 603 Sqn Spitfire (the *Geschwader*'s old adversaries from its Battle of Britain days!)

On the ground, meanwhile, a number of developments were taking place. On 18 January the *Geschwader*'s strength was bolstered by the temporary attachment of II./JG 3. At about the same time, I./JG 53 – which appears not to have engaged in any operations at all over Malta during January – was split up, with part of its strength being ordered inland from Gela to San Pietro. Here, in the latter half of the month, it was instrumental in establishing a new fighter-bomber *Staffel*.

Commanded by Oberleutnant Werner Langemann, 10.(*Jabo*)/JG 53's pilots were a mix of old and new. Preference was, of course, given to those with previous fighter-bomber experience, such as Unteroffizier Felix Sauer, who had flown with 3./JG 53 during the Battle of Britain. But when a call went out to the other *Gruppen* for personnel, it did not always produce those of the highest calibre – it is an age-old military truism that unit commanders will invariably take full advantage of such appeals to unload those subordinates they would most like to be rid off. Finally, there was a third category of pilot making up the *Staffel* – a cadre of NCOs straight from training school.

Despite these differences, the *Kapitän* soon welded his command into a cohesive whole, its new sense of identity being proclaimed by a large sign on the ops room wall – 'Langemann & Co. Ltd. – Bomb Exporters'.

While I./JG 53 was setting up the *Jabostaffel* at San Pietro, its own 1. *Staffel* spent some time on temporary detachment to airfields in Greece and Crete, protecting those transport units flying supplies to North Africa across the eastern Mediterranean. And in the third week of January the weather over Sicily at last began to show distinct signs of improvement, allowing the island's waterlogged airfields to start drying out. Having been re-equipped with new *Friedrichs* since returning from Libya the previous month, III./JG 53 flew its first Malta operation – inevitably a Ju 88 escort mission – on 19 January. This passed without due incident, unlike a similar

65

Major von Maltzahn (centre)
is interviewed at Comiso by
a Luftwaffe war correspondent
(at right, holding microphone) as
German and Italian officers look on.
Note the *Regia Aeronautica* Macchi
C.202 in the background to right

sortie undertaken by the *Geschwaderstab* six days later, which developed into the fiercest air battle yet fought by the 'Ace of Spades' over Malta.

The briefed target for the four Ju 88s being escorted by *Stab* JG 53's five fighters on that 25 January 1942 is believed to have been Hal Far airfield. But as the small force approached the southeastern tip of Malta, they chanced upon two supply vessels being shepherded away from the island under an aerial umbrella of some dozen Hurricanes. The first of the British fighters hardly had time to open fire on the Junkers before the Bf 109s fell upon them. A war correspondent who was visiting Comiso at the time interviewed Major von Maltzahn upon the *Stab*'s return to base, and the *Kommodore*'s own account of the action subsequently appeared in newspapers throughout the Reich;

'Concerned at first about being spotted, I led my five machines round in a wide curve to the rear so that I could make my initial attack on the five Hurricanes from astern out of the sun. The move paid off. We closed in unnoticed and I lined up on the outermost left-hand Hurricane. It was hit, immediately went down and crashed into the sea in flames. I then gathered my *Schwarm* together again and prepared for a second attack.

'The Hurricanes turned towards land and tried to climb above us. I allowed myself a little time, so that my machines would be able to make a concerted attack. At this point I saw two of the twelve somewhat higher Hurricanes begin to curve around with the obvious intention of getting on our tails. But they didn't do so, flying off towards the coast instead. This enabled me to carry out the second attack undisturbed.

'Once again I took the left outermost machine so that my comrades could also get into firing position. Again the Hurricane took a direct hit. The pilot bailed out. I saw him fall frighteningly close past my cabin roof. At the same time two other Mes were attacking another pair of enemy machines, which were also shot own and hit the ground in flames. That made it three more kills.

'The other machines dived away in an attempt to escape from us, and they succeeded, but they then had the misfortune to bump into the fighter escort of another bomber formation, whereupon two more Hurricanes went down on fire into the sea. Another pair spun down leaving banners of black smoke behind them, but they were not seen to crash. Lt P (Leutnant Karl-Heinz Preu), on the other hand, chased a Hurricane almost as far as the coast, where he caught up with and shot it down just off-shore from an altitude of 600 metres. That was victory number eight.'

In all, the *Geschwaderstab* was credited with six kills, the *Kommodore's* first two – which took his total to 55 – being confirmed by his wing-mounted gun camera. The remaining pair were claimed by pilots of 6. *Staffel*, who had been escorting the other formation of Ju 88s. With neither unit suffering any casualties, it was one of the *Geschwader's* most successful days of the campaign against Malta.

Forty-eight hours later, on 27 January, another pilot of 6./JG 53 – Oberleutnant Helmut Belser, who had already claimed a highly suspect 'Gloster Gladiator' (more likely a Fleet Air Arm Swordfish or Albacore) on 19 January – was credited with an even more unlikely 'Fairey Battle'. If Belser's aircraft recognition was not completely at fault, this latter may have been another naval machine – the superficially similar Fairey Fulmar. And, curiously enough, there *had* been a Fulmar aloft over Malta on that date, but this had been a war-weary example that had staggered into the air from Hal Far shortly after dawn, heading for North Africa, whereas Belser's 'Battle' was claimed in the late afternoon.

6. *Staffel* seemed to have a penchant for adding exotic types to its scoreboard. The Wellington downed off Malta on the morning of 5 February at the end of a long delivery flight from Gibraltar was not exactly uncommon (nor was it shot down, but merely damaged). Leutnant Hans Möller may have been interested to learn, however, that the twin-engined floatplane he destroyed at its moorings at Kalfrana later that day – and which he identified as a Dutch Fokker T VIII – was, in fact, a German-built machine, being one of three ex-Norwegian air force Heinkel He 115s that the RAF used for covert operations in the Mediterranean.

February had brought with it clear blue skies, and a corresponding increase in Luftwaffe activity over Malta. And although missions became more frequent, each remained on a small scale. It was thought that a constant succession of minor raids and alarms – by day and by night – would be far more effective in wearing down the island's defenders than a series of heavier all-out attacks that could only be mounted at intervals, leaving the RAF with valuable breathing space between each.

Escorting the daylight bombers to Malta and back became JG 53's

Leutnant Karl-Heinz Preu (right) of the *Geschwaderstab* is pictured with *Kommodore* von Maltzahn in front of the latter's *Friedrich* in its substantial, stone-built blast pen at Comiso. Fully recovered from the wound to his left arm suffered in Russia, 'Bob' Preu would be killed over Malta on 7 July 1942 – although sources differ as to whether he fell victim to anti-aircraft fire or the island's top-scoring ace, Canadian Plt Off George 'Screwball' Beurling of No 249 Sqn

Oberleutnant Klaus Quaet-Faslem, *Staffelkapitän* of 2./JG 53, scored three (numbers eight to ten) of the 41 victories he gained while with the *Geschwader* during I. *Gruppe*'s first tour of duty in the Mediterranean against Malta. Made *Gruppenkommandeur* of I./JG 3 in August 1942, he took his final total to 49, before being lost during Defence of the Reich operations on 30 January 1944

9. *Staffel*'s Unteroffizier Gerhard Beitz returns to Comiso after just having claimed his first victory – one of the four Hurricanes downed by III./JG 53 over Malta on 9 March 1942. Beitz would add a second (a Spitfire) on 18 May in an action which ended when he himself bailed out of his 'Yellow 2' into British captivity

primary duty. Interspersed with the occasional *Jabo* escort mission and *freie Jagd* sweep, the *Geschwader*'s pilots found themselves flying anything from two to five sorties a day. It developed almost into a routine – rendezvous with the Junkers above the airfield, accompany them on the 15-20 minute flight to Malta, protect them over the target area, see them safely home again. And it appeared to be working, as Luftwaffe pilots and crews reported a noticeable decline in the island's aerial defences.

During February, JG 53 claimed 24 aircraft destroyed at a cost to itself of just two pilots missing. But the successes were by no means evenly distributed throughout the *Geschwader*. While the *Stabsschwarm* added seven to its total, including four more for the *Kommodore*, I. *Gruppe*, after its January sabbatical, managed just one – a Beaufort credited to Oberleutnant Klaus Quaet-Faslem, *Staffelkapitän* of 2./JG 53, on 15 February.

II. *Gruppe* was alone responsible for almost half of February's kills (12 of the 25), but also suffered the month's first combat casualty when a 6. *Staffel* pilot fell victim to anti-aircraft fire close to Luqa on 7 February. III./JG 53 gained its first five victories since returning from its African adventure, starting with a Blenheim downed by 8. *Staffel*'s *Kapitän*, Oberleutnant Hans-Joachim Heinecke, on 11 February. And it was 10.(*Jabo*)/JG 53 which sustained the month's second loss on the 23rd – just two days after the *Staffel*'s operational debut – when one of its NCO pilots was declared missing after being shot down into the sea off Malta by Hurricanes. German records state that the aircraft ditched northeast of the island, while RAF combat reports describe the pilot's bailing out.

March began in very much the same way as February had ended. The *Geschwader* claimed nine Hurricanes in as many days against the single loss of another *Jabostaffel* machine (its pilot being captured after being downed by ground fire). The Axis air forces were now within hours, it seemed, of achieving their aim of neutralising Malta. The island's defences were in a desperate state, with less than two-dozen serviceable Hurricanes remaining. But on 10 March the *Geschwader* was in for a surprise.

Three days earlier, apparently unnoticed by German intelligence, a small force of 15 Spitfires had been flown onto the island from the deck of the Royal Navy carrier HMS *Eagle*. The first pilots of JG 53 to

encounter the new British fighters were members of 8. *Staffel*, escorting a trio of Ju 88s in an attack on Luqa. Honours on this 10 March were even, with one *Friedrich* lost and one Spitfire destroyed. But the writing was clearly on the wall. If this first batch of Spitfires had got through, others would no doubt attempt to follow (in fact, another 16 would be flown off the *Eagle* and arrive in Malta before the end of the month).

It was perhaps no coincidence that Generalfeldmarschall Albert Kesselring, GOC *Luftflotte* 2, called a conference of his unit commanders at Catania on 12 March to spell out the future conduct of the offensive against Malta. In order to eliminate the threat posed by the island once and for all, large-scale bombing raids – aimed particularly at the enemy's airfields – would be flown before the RAF could rebuild its strength. It was to take a good week to put these orders into effect, during which time the *Geschwader* reportedly accounted for six more Spitfires.

The first major daylight bombing raids of this latest phase in the battle for Malta were launched on the morning of 21 March, when 100+ Ju 88s attacked Takali airfield. JG 53, which had been flying more and more *freie Jagd* sorties of late, put up a maximum effort to provide the Junkers with the strongest possible fighter escort. But it encountered no aerial opposition over the island and the day passed without either victory or loss. It did, however, set the pattern for the coming month. Throughout the next four weeks the entire *Geschwader* – with the obvious exception of the *Jabostaffel* – was engaged almost exclusively in escorting large numbers of bombers as they shuttled back and forth between Sicily and Malta.

Although slightly recovered (by the infusion of Spitfires), the island's aerial defences were still far from adequate. Taking full advantage, the

Back from another mission over Malta in March 1942, Hauptmann Herbert Kaminski (centre), the *Kommandeur* of I./JG 53, and two of his pilots seek shelter from the glaring Gela sun as they make straight for the shade of the ops room building

Despite pulling off this neat belly landing – the result of engine failure – on a Sicilian beach on 27 March, Unteroffizier Felix Sauer's 'White 3' had to be written-off due to salt water corrosion. Note the 10. *Jabostaffel* badge – a bomb striking the island of Malta, superimposed on the aft fuselage white theatre band (compare with colour profile 19)

Oberleutnant Gerhard Michalski, *Kapitän* of 4./JG 53, returns from yet another mission over Malta – possibly that of 2 April, when he claimed a Spitfire. He would emerge as the *Geschwader's* top scorer in operations against the island, during which he amassed 26 of the 68 victories he was to achieve with JG 53. He ended the war as *Kommodore* of JG 4, with the Oak Leaves and a final total of 73

*Geschwader's* combat kill-to-loss ratio during this period climbed to nearly 10-to-1. It was credited with 39 enemy aircraft destroyed for the loss of one pilot killed, two missing and one captured – although two more *Jabostaffel* pilots were declared missing after being involved in a mid-air collision over the sea.

Over half the total number of victories fell to Hauptmann Walter Spies' II./JG 53. Its most successful day occurred on 10 April when the *Gruppe* claimed six Hurricanes during a late afternoon escort mission. Among the six was one credited to the *Gruppenkommandeur* himself, plus a trio for future Knight's Cross winner Oberfeldwebel Rudolf Ehrenberger of 6. *Staffel* (taking his current score to 23). But the same action also resulted in the loss of Ehrenberger's *Staffelkapitän*.

At Comiso, Leutnant Hermann Neuhoff had been moved across from III. *Gruppe* to take command of 6./JG 53 only 24 hours earlier. With 39 kills to his credit (a 40th had been disallowed on the day of his transfer), Neuhoff was III. *Gruppe's* top scorer. Uncertainty surrounds the exact circumstances of his loss. Although two RAF pilots claimed a Bf 109 over eastern Malta – with, in each case, the enemy fighter bursting into flames and its pilot baling out – Hermann Neuhoff later subscribed to the generally held German belief that he had, in fact, been the victim of 'friendly fire' – shot down by another Messerschmitt;

'I was leading my *Schwarm* over Malta when three Spitfires appeared. I opened fire at a machine in front of me. At the same moment there was an almighty bang. Lt Schöw had just scored his first kill – unfortunately it was I. He had mistaken me for a Hurricane.

'I remained in my machine. But when it began to burn ever more fiercely, I released the canopy. Shortly afterwards the '109 exploded. It was lucky that I had unfastened my harness and jettisoned the cockpit hood. I was thrown out of the aircraft at an altitude of 2500 metres, deployed my 'chute at about 400 metres and made a "belly-landing" not far from Luqa.'

Taken into captivity, the award of the Knight's Cross to Leutnant Hermann Neuhoff – the *Geschwader's* ninth – would be announced on 16 June. Less than two months later, on 11 August 1942, the hapless Leutnant Werner Schöw of 1./JG 53, who had immediately admitted to firing at a Messerschmitt 'in the heat of the battle', would be reported missing on the Stalingrad front with a final score of 15 (excluding Neuhoff's 'Yellow 1'?).

Four days after Hermann Neuhoff went down over Malta, II./JG 53 lost a second high-scoring *Staffelkapitän* – albeit in a far less controversial manner – when 5./JG 53's 34-victory Hauptmann Kurt Brändle was appointed *Gruppenkommandeur* of II./JG 3.

With a bemused Italian officer looking on, two leutnants of 9. *Staffel*, Wolf Schaller (left) and Hermann Munzert (right), ham it up at Comiso in the spring of 1942. The 11-victory Schaller would not long survive III. *Gruppe*'s return to Africa, being shot down by a Hurricane near El Alamein on 12 July. Hermann Munzert – having in the meantime been appointed *Staffelkapitän* of 2./JG 53, and with 20 kills to his credit, was wounded in action against B-17s over Tunisia on 31 January 1943 and succumbed to his injuries six days later

During the latter half of April the bombing offensive against Malta reached its climax. On 20 April, 46 more Spitfires were flown in to the beleaguered island from the aircraft carriers HMS *Eagle* and USS *Wasp*. This time, however, the Germans were aware of Allied intentions. Almost as soon as the reinforcements had touched down, the airfields of Hal Far and Takali were subjected to severe bombing raids. The following morning little more than half of the newly arrived Spitfires remained operational.

It was therefore not the uncertain trickle of fresh men and machines that brought temporary relief to the defenders of Malta at the end of April 1942. The real reason behind the easing of the aerial bombardment was the Wehrmacht's own operational commitments elsewhere. Hitler was preparing to launch his summer offensive on the eastern front, and in North Africa Rommel was again on the attack. Having fought his way back to the Gazala line (the scene of III. *Gruppe*'s withdrawal in December 1941), he was now planning to recapture Tobruk and advance into Egypt.

By this mid-point of the war the Luftwaffe's resources were already becoming dangerously overstretched. It was having difficulty meeting the many operational demands made upon it. Established units were being split and their component elements sent to entirely different fronts.

And nowhere was this more apparent than within the ranks of JG 53. For while Major von Maltzahn's *Geschwaderstab* and II. *Gruppe* would initially remain together at Comiso, in Sicily, to keep up some semblance of pressure on Malta, Hauptmann Herbert Kaminski's I./JG 53 was soon to find itself accompanying 6. *Armee* in its march on Stalingrad, while III./JG 53 would be sent back across the Mediterranean to its old stamping grounds around Derna, in Libya, as part of the air component being readied to cover the *Afrika Korps'* forthcoming advance on Cairo.

Oberleutnant Franz Götz, having taken over as the *Kapitän* of 9. *Staffel* at the height of the Battle of Britain, was by now an experienced *alte Hase* ('old hare') who fully recognised the benefit of grabbing 40 winks whenever the opportunity arose

# THE PARTING OF THE WAYS

When the bombing of Malta was scaled down at the end of April 1942, Major Herbert Kaminski's I./JG 53 were ordered to pass its aircraft over to other *Gruppen* based in Sicily and return to the Reich for rest and refit. It would remain at Schwäbisch-Hall, northeast of Stuttgart, for the best part of a month before departing for the eastern front. Staging via Prague and Zhitomir, the unit arrived at Kursk, in the central sector, on 29 May.

From here it would take part in Operation *Blau* (Blue), the opening stage of the summer 1942 offensive aimed at conquering all of southern Russia. The pilots' initial task would be to cover the armoured divisions of 4. *Panzerarmee*, which formed the left-hand pincer of a giant encircling movement planned to trap the Red Army units defending Voronezh on the River Don.

But the offensive was not scheduled to begin until 28 June. In the meantime, the *Gruppe* quickly re-adapted to life on the eastern front, which the longer-serving among the unit's pilots had last experienced in August 1941. One enemy activity they had not had to contend with the previous summer was the almost nightly nuisance raids on their airfield by light biplanes of the Soviet Air Force – 'sewing machines' in the Luftwaffe vernacular. It was during one such harassment attack on 2 June that the *Gruppe* suffered its first casualty when 1. *Staffel*'s Oberleutnant Udo Padior was fatally wounded by bomb splinters.

In the air, however, pilots were soon achieving success on an unprecedented scale, even outstripping their performance during the heady opening days of *Barbarossa*. The *Gruppe* had returned to Russia at a low ebb, as its recent four-month stay on Sicily had netted only 19 victories. Oberleutnant Wolfgang Tonne, whose 3. *Staffel* had been responsible for just one out of that unimpressive total, was on the point of resigning his command.

All that was to change when I./JG 53 flew its first missions early on the morning of 31 May and nine enemy aircraft were brought down, all by 3. *Staffel* – six by Oberleutnant Tonne alone. It was the start of an amazing string of successes which, in the space of just four months (the same length of time, coincidentally, as the *Gruppe*'s recent Sicilian sojourn), would see Tonne's score climb from 14 to 100. He would be awarded the Knight's Cross and the Oak Leaves for this outstanding effort. Nor was he to be the only one to be decorated during this period.

By the time I./JG 53 transferred forward to Kolpna, some 50 kilometres northeast of Kursk, on 24 June, its pilots had already added a further 42 victories to their collective scoreboard. Four days later, with the launch of Operation *Blau*, they claimed 14 kills in the course of six missions flown between dawn and dusk. Leutnant Joachim Louis, the *Gruppen-Adjutant*,

The first *Gustavs* to wear the 'Ace of Spades' badge were the Bf 109G-2s with which I./JG 53 were re-equipped in the Ukraine in mid-July 1942 . . .

. . . before commencing operations in the southern sector of the eastern front later that same month. Here, 2. *Staffel*'s 'Black 3' receives some last-minute attention from its groundcrew. Note the broad yellow band aft of the fuselage cross denoting the Russian front

had been credited with four of them, all LaGG-3s. Louis then got the sole victory of 29 June, and the only two successes of the day after that. These latter had taken his total to 22, but his own machine was also hit in the same dogfight some 25 kilometres behind enemy lines. Joachim Louis parachuted into six long years of Soviet captivity.

On 10 July I./JG 53 retired to Uman, in the Ukraine, to re-equip with Bf 109G-2s – thus becoming the first *Gruppe* within the *Geschwader* to receive *Gustavs* – before then transferring to Kharkov for nine days' familiarisation on their new mounts. These moves had taken them into the southern sector of the front, and on 24 July they headed further south still to Taganrog, on the shores of the Sea of Azov.

It was upon arriving at Taganrog that the *Gruppenkommandeur*, who had reported engine problems earlier in the transfer flight, suddenly announced that he had to make an emergency landing.

Inexplicably selecting a small airfield on the northern outskirts, rather than the city's main air base (the *Gruppe*'s actual destination), Major Herbert Kaminski came in too fast in a steep left turn. The brand new *Gustav* broke up on impact, shedding engine and wings, while the fuselage careered on for another 90 metres or more. The injured Kaminski – who had won the Knight's Cross while serving with a *Zerstörergruppe* – was rushed to hospital, where he made a speedy recovery. But the incident lent credence to *Kommodore* 'Henri' Maltzahn's initial assessment of Kaminski when he had first arrived to take command of I. *Gruppe* eight months earlier;

'A splendid fellow, but not the world's best fighter pilot.'

Hauptmann Walter Spies, long-serving *Kommandeur* of II./JG 53, flew in from Sicily to take Kaminski's place. And it was under his leadership that I. *Gruppe*, having moved forward to a field near Tazinskaya on

26 July, embarked upon possibly the most successful eight weeks of its entire history as it covered 6. *Armee*'s fateful advance on Stalingrad.

I./JG 53 had been credited with 19 victories on the day of its transfer to Tazinskaya, but the unit's rapidly lengthening scoreboard was not achieved entirely without casualties. On 1 August – by which time the *Gruppe* had leapfrogged forward yet again to Frolov, a hastily prepared landing strip on the River Chir, to the southeast of Stalingrad – it lost its first *Gustavs* in combat when two 1. *Staffel* machines were shot down in a dogfight with half-a-dozen LaGG-3s east of the Don.

In fact, not everybody was enamoured with the Bf 109G. The new model's more powerful engine was, to a large extent, offset by the increase in the *Gustav*'s all-up weight. Nor was its armament all it might be. An attempt was made to improve firepower by the addition of two extra 20 mm cannon in underwing gondolas. But, again, the few machines so converted did not find favour with all. There were exceptions, however – Wolfgang Tonne in particular, used the so-called 'gunboat' to devastating effect against the enemy both in the air and on the ground.

On 4 August the *Gruppe* moved to Bereska, on the River Don. By now it had become the norm for each pilot to fly three or four missions a day – on some occasions they even undertook six or seven. But the many recent moves had exposed the fragility of their supply situation. Food and fuel were running dangerously short, and this, combined with the natural conditions of the southern Russian steppe baking under a summer sun – the heat, the dust and the mosquitoes – all added to their operational burden. But still they continued to bring down large numbers of the enemy. All but four of the 18 victories claimed on 5 August went to Oberleutnant Tonne's 3. *Staffel*.

On 8 August air activity grew even more intense when the Red Army units defending the Don, the last natural river barrier before Stalingrad, were encircled in the final great 'cauldron' battle of the eastern front campaign. In four days I./JG 53's pilots were credited with a further 60 machines destroyed. But it cost them four of their own, including 1. *Staffel*'s Leutnant Werner Schöw – he of the Neuhoff 'incident' over Malta – who was reported missing after his 'White 4' was hit in the radiator and crashed during a dogfight near Stalingrad on 11 August.

The following day was something of a milestone, for among the 27 successes credited to the *Gruppe* on that 12 August were the 60th for Wolfgang Tonne and half-centuries for both 'Tutti' Müller and Walter Zellot. And while these three were the undisputed top-ranking trio of I./JG 53's *Experten* at this time, there were many others within the *Gruppe* who were also adding significantly to their totals at the expense of the Red Air Force units barring the way to Stalingrad.

Among those chasing the leading scorers were both *'Alte Hasen'* – 'old hares', or veterans – and tyros alike. Oberleutnant Klaus Quaet-Faslem, the *Kapitän* of 2. *Staffel*, for example (whose two victories on 12 August raised his tally to 33) had claimed his first kill over Poland in September 1939. 3. *Staffel*'s Unteroffizier Wilhelm Crinius, on the other hand, with a trio of MiG-3s downed on 12 August taking him to 28, had scored his first two victories (a pair of heavily armoured *Sturmoviks*) little more than eight weeks earlier, shortly after the *Gruppe*'s arrival at Kursk.

On 19 August 'Quat' Quaet-Faslem was appointed *Kommandeur* of I./JG 3, a *Jagdgruppe* that was currently sharing I./JG 53's base at Tusow – an airfield in the Don Bend some 65 miles due west of Stalingrad. He was replaced at the head of 2./JG 53 by Leutnant Walter Zellot. This meant that the *Gruppe's* three most successful pilots were now also its three *Staffelkapitäne*. And, as formation leaders, they had ample opportunities to add yet further to their individual totals. This they proceeded to do over the course of the next few days in the areas to the south and east of Stalingrad as ground forces prepared to launch the final assault on the city.

By the end of the month German troops had reached the outer suburbs. But the Red Army held on desperately. The pilots of I./JG 53 were at full stretch providing escorts for the relays of bombers and Stukas pounding the Soviet positions, flying ground attack missions and protecting their own forward units. These efforts did not go unrewarded, as September would bring with it a whole flurry of decorations.

The first went to Leutnant Walter Zellot, the recently appointed *Kapitän* of 2. *Staffel*, who was awarded the Knight's Cross on 3 September for a reported 84 victories (although his actual total on that date was 78). Three days later Oberleutnant Wolfgang Tonne was similarly honoured for his then score of 73.

But there was another side to the coin. On 9 September – a day on which 'Tutti' Müller convincingly demonstrated his prowess on the 'gunboat' by downing no fewer than six *Sturmoviks* – 2. *Staffel's* Oberfeldwebel Alfred Franke was reported missing in action (also against *Sturmoviks*). The 59-victory Franke would receive a posthumous Knight's Cross late the following month. And 24 hours after Franke's loss, Walter Zellot was killed during a low-level attack on Soviet troops northwest of Stalingrad when the tail of his *Gustav* was blown off by anti-aircraft fire (some sources suggest Zellot may have been the victim of German flak).

Despite the spectacular successes of its top half-dozen scorers, who had been credited with the majority of the 85 victories claimed by the *Gruppe* in the three days leading up to 10 September (when it moved to Pitomnik, less than 12 miles from the centre of Stalingrad), I./JG 53 was inevitably beginning to suffer under the strain of such prolonged operational activity.

Pictured in the company of Gerhard Michalski, Hauptmann Friedrich-Karl Müller (right), the *Staffelkapitän* of 1./JG 53, wears the Oak Leaves awarded on 23 September 1942 for topping the century mark

Walter Zellot was not replaced immediately, his 2. *Staffel* instead being temporarily amalgamated with 1./JG 53 under the command of Hauptmann Friedrich-Karl Müller.

And it was 'Tutti' Müller's two kills of 19 September that took his total to 101, and would earn him one of the three sets of Oak Leaves about to be awarded to the *Gruppe*. For hot on Müller's heels were the *Kapitän* of 3. *Staffel*, Oberleutnant Wolfgang Tonne, and his highest-scoring pilot, Feldwebel Crinius, both of whom were currently tied at 96 victories each. Putting aside their friendly rivalry, *Staffelkapitän* and

Fellow *Staffelkapitän* Oberleutnant Wolfgang Tonne of 3./JG 53 was not far behind 'Tutti' Müller. The rudder of his Bf 109G-2 already displays 95 victories – the first five were gained in the west and the remainder came on the eastern front. Nos 92-95 were claimed in the Stalingrad area on 18 September. Müller would reach his century four days later

It is said that the camera does not lie, but it can confuse. This photograph shows a winter-camouflaged *Gustav* of I. *Gruppe* on the Stalingrad front towards the end of 1942 . . . or does it? The 'Ace of Spades' is clearly in evidence, but I./JG 53 was withdrawn from Russia late in September, when the temperature was admittedly already dropping but the first heavy snows had yet to fall. The answer can be found in that vertical III. *Gruppe* bar just visible on the machine's rear fuselage – this is one of the G-2s left behind by I./JG 53 and subsequently handed over to another unit (almost certainly III./JG 3, which operated out of Pitomnik from September to November 1942)

NCO agreed to fly together and try to get their centuries on the same day – which they did on 22 September.

23 September thus witnessed not only the award of the Oak Leaves to Hauptmann Friedrich-Karl Müller, but also Feldwebel Crinius' receiving both his Knight's Cross *and* the Oak Leaves on the same date. For some unknown reason Oberleutnant Tonne's Oak Leaves were not announced until 24 hours later.

By this time the weather had turned appreciably colder, and the Red Army was already beginning to probe that sector of the front north of Stalingrad held by Axis satellite troops. Both were ominous signs – the temperature was about to plunge, and it was against the Rumanians that the Soviets would launch their massive counter-attack that would ultimately lead to the encirclement of Stalingrad and the annihilation of the 6. *Armee*.

But I./JG 53 was not to be part of the unfolding tragedy. On 25 September the *Gruppe* claimed its last seven victories over Stalingrad (including four Yak-1s for 3. *Staffel*'s Unteroffizier Heinz Golinski). That same day I./JG 3 flew in to Pitomnik to relieve it. The *Gruppe* passed its remaining *Gustavs* over to the newcomers on 27 September before embarking on the long journey by road, rail and air to Comiso in Sicily.

At a cost to itself of fewer than 20 pilots killed, missing or captured, I./JG 53's second expedition to the eastern front had resulted in an amazing 900+ victories – a success ratio of more than 45-to-1.

When I. *Gruppe* had first departed Sicily at the beginning of May 1942, it had left its aircraft behind and been flown north to Germany for re-equipment, prior to transferring to Russia. When III./JG 53 vacated Comiso three weeks later, it was

flying its own *Friedrichs* and heading not north, but south, back across the Mediterranean to Libya, where the unit had already seen brief service in December 1941.

The two *Gruppen* did have one thing in common, however. Both were supporting renewed advances by the ground troops – 6.*Armee*'s drive to capture Stalingrad, and the *Afrika Korps*' push through Egypt to cut the Suez Canal. What they could not know at the time, of course, was that neither objective would be attained. The two advances would prove to be the last significant territorial gains ever achieved by the Wehrmacht. Both would be rapidly forfeited again. And thereafter JG 53's war would be one of almost unremitting withdrawal and retreat, its only purpose then serving to defer the inevitable defeat of the Third Reich for as long as possible.

Just before leaving Sicily, III./JG 53 had lost its *Kommandeur* of nearly two years' standing when Hauptmann Wolf-Dietrich Wilcke was appointed *Geschwaderkommodore* of JG 3. The *Gruppe*'s new commander was awaiting it upon the unit's arrival at Martuba, in Libya, on 25 May. He was Major Erich Gerlitz, previously *Gruppenkommandeur* of the resident II./JG 27. And it was under JG 27 – the famed 'Afrika' *Geschwader* – that the 'Ace of Spades' pilots would be operating in the weeks ahead.

Those weeks were to see III./JG 53 move base nearly a dozen times as the *Afrika Korps* first smashed through the Gazala Line, took Tobruk, and then advanced into Egypt.

On 27 May, the day after General Rommel launched his assault on the Gazala defences, the *Gruppe* achieved its first success when its current top scorer, 9. *Staffel*'s Oberfeldwebel Werner Stumpf, was credited with a solitary P-40 southeast of El Adem. And 72 hours later it very nearly suffered its first casualty when the *Kapitän* of 7. *Staffel* was accidentally brought down by fire from a Ju 88. Oberleutnant Wilfried Pufahl managed to pull off an emergency landing away from base, however, and was back in the air the following day to claim one of six P-40s that fell to the *Gruppe* on that 31 May.

In the first half of June, as the air fighting continued to rage above the Gazala battlefield, III./JG 53 accounted for another 18 Allied fighters. On 12 June it was joined at Martuba by the *Friedrichs* of Oberleutnant Langemann's 10.(*Jabo*)/JG 53. The newcomers were to be subordinated

I./JG 53 may have avoided the winter snows of Russia, but III. *Gruppe* could not escape the all-pervading sand and dust of North Africa. 9. *Staffel*'s 'Yellow 9' kicks up clouds of the stuff as it taxies out at the start of another mission

to the *Gruppe* for their forthcoming fighter-bomber operations in direct support of Rommel's advancing ground troops, for on 14 June Commonwealth forces had at last begun pulling back from Gazala.

But on that date the pilots of III./JG 53 were busy elsewhere – out over the Mediterranean escorting bombers and Stukas attacking a westbound supply convoy from Alexandria that was attempting to get through to Malta. They claimed five of the convoy's fighter umbrella, later adding a Hudson and a Beaufighter to bring their day's collective total to seven.

The convoy from Egypt was just one half of a determined Allied effort to revictual Malta. At the same time other ships were heading east from the Straits of Gibraltar. The two convoys were intended to reach Malta on successive days. It would appear that German intelligence had again got wind of their opponents' plans. On 15 June, as part of the Axis response, III./JG 53 was ordered to return, via Greece, post-haste to Malta.

On the first leg of its flight across the eastern Mediterranean, however, the *Gruppe* chanced upon a large formation of twin-engined aircraft which its pilots initially took to be part of the convoy's escort. In fact, the enemy machines were a strike force of Beaufort torpedo-bombers, escorted by Beaufighters, hunting for units of the Italian fleet reported to be in the vicinity. In a confused series of actions just over 80 miles north-northeast of Derna – almost midway between the coast of Africa and Crete – Gerlitz's pilots claimed eight Beauforts and a brace of Beaufighters for the *Gruppe*'s most successful day of their entire 'desert' war!

After the encounter, with insufficient fuel to reach their intended destination in Greece, part of the *Gruppe* put down at Maleme, on the island of Crete, where it would stay for the next few days.

In the meantime, the ground campaign in North Africa was gathering pace. Lunging forward from Gazala, Rommel's troops attacked Tobruk on 20 June. The fortress port, which had withstood an eight-month siege in 1941, fell in just one day. Commonwealth forces then retreated back on El Alamein, an obscure halt on the coastal railway heading west out of Alexandria, where they prepared to make a last-ditch stand. Crossing the border into Egypt, the now Generalfeldmarschall Rommel tried to take the El Alamein position 'on the run', but failed after a series of frontal assaults that lasted throughout the first week of July.

An unfortunately somewhat damaged print of a pair of 7. *Staffel* Bf 109F-4s on patrol over the Libyan-Egyptian border region. 'White 1' in the foreground wears the new desert tan/light blue camouflage scheme. As it was still very much the custom in III. *Gruppe* at this time for the aircraft of *Staffelkapitäne* to carry the numeral '1', this may well be the mount of ten-victory Hauptmann Wilfried Pufahl, who would be transferred to a training unit in early 1943

III./JG 53 had followed the *Afrika Korps* into Egypt, staging via Gambut, east of Tobruk, first to Sidi Barrani and then to Quotaifiya, only some 43 miles short of El Alamein. Arriving on 1 July, this would be its base for much of the next four months while the exhausted ground forces – Axis and Commonwealth alike – sought to rebuild their strength for the final, and deciding, battle for North Africa.

Throughout this entire period, from mid-June until early October, the highest number of enemy machines claimed by *Gruppe* pilots on any one day was just three. And even this was achieved only once. More often than not it was just a single kill that they were able to add to their daily total – and then usually only with an interval of several days, or even as much as week, in between. Fortunately, their casualties were also kept within acceptable limits. But they did include two *Staffelkapitäne*.

It was on 19 June that 8./JG 53's Hauptmann Helmut Belser had been killed in a take-off accident at Castel Benito during a ferry flight. The 36-victory Belser would be honoured with a posthumous Knight's Cross on 6 September. By that time his replacement had also been lost, for after becoming involved in a dogfight with P-40s during a *freie Jagd* sweep over El Alamein on 3 July, Oberleutnant Ernst Klager was shot down and captured.

In August III./JG 53 bade farewell to its fighter-bombers when Oberleutnant Werner Langemann's 10.(*Jabo*)/JG 53 was combined with 10.(*Jabo*)/JG 27 to form the two-*Staffel* strong *Jabogruppe Afrika*. During its desert operations the *Staffel* had been credited with one victory – a Hurricane claimed by the *Kapitän* himself on 5 July. The unit also suffered one loss when a pilot bailed out into captivity after his machine was hit by anti-aircraft fire south of El Alamein on 15 August.

Although III./JG 53's top scorers could not compete in terms of numbers of enemy aircraft destroyed with the incredible totals being racked up by the pilots of I. *Gruppe* on the road to Stalingrad, their achievements in the desert did not go unrecognised. The two leading

This desert dump overrun by the advancing 8th Army was the last resting place for a number of III. *Gruppe*'s machines, including 'Yellow 2' of 9. *Staffel* on the right. Note too, beyond the Bf 110 of ZG 26 in the foreground, the remains of 10.(*Jabo*)/JG 53's 'White 10', still bearing the unit's 'bomb striking Malta' badge on a broad white aft fuselage band

79

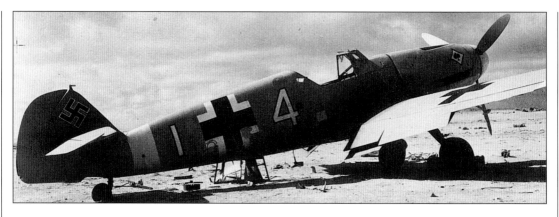

**9.** *Staffel's* 'Yellow 4' has apparently come to a lonelier end, abandoned on a deserted forward landing strip, its canopy – complete with armoured headrest – lying on the ground beside it. Note the oversized fuselage cross, minus outer black edging, which was a not uncommon feature on desert-camouflaged *Friedrichs*

*Experten*, both of 9. *Staffel*, each received the Knight's Cross after attaining 40 kills. The first had been awarded to Oberfeldwebel Werner Stumpf on 13 August (by which time his tally had risen to 42). The second went to *Staffelkapitän* Oberleutnant Franz Götz on 4 September. His 40th had been a Spitfire shot down during a Stuka escort mission on 22 July.

Despite the *Gruppe's* claiming ten kills in September – including a Boston encountered during a long-range intruder mission to Cairo – for the loss of only one of its own pilots (forced-landed and captured during the same Cairo mission on 27th), it was becoming clear that the British were winning the supplies race. And when heavy rains flooded most of the Luftwaffe's forward fighter fields on 9 October, the Allies mounted an all-out effort to try to destroy the Axis air forces on the ground.

Under appalling conditions, and near constant bombardment from the air throughout the day, III./JG 53's pilots managed to fly at least four separate sorties on this date, during the course of which they were credited with bringing down nine P-40s – the first such multiple daily total since the 'massacre of the Beauforts' out over the Mediterranean on 15 June. However, they were unable to prevent the destruction of their ops room and 13 of their *Friedrichs* on the ground at Quotaifiya. Fortunately, there was only one casualty – a 7. *Staffel* pilot slightly wounded during a strafing attack.

A more serious loss was suffered four days later when Oberfeldwebel Werner Stumpf, who had been sporting his Knight's Cross for exactly two months, became the latest victim of El Alamein's anti-aircraft defences. Stumpf had been responsible for the first victory of the *Gruppe's* present African 'tour' – the single P-40 downed on 27 May. Future Knight's Cross recipient Leutnant Jürgen Harder was credited with the 107th, and last, when he claimed III./JG 53's sole success of 26 October – another P-40. During the intervening five months the *Gruppe* had lost eight pilots killed or missing in action, plus three captured.

On the night of 23 October, Gen Montgomery opened the Battle of El Alamein with the greatest concentrated artillery barrage of the war to date. Axis forces clung on desperately, and it was not until 4 November that Rommel finally issued the order to withdraw. By that time, however, III./JG 53 was already back in Sicily. After completing their last missions on 27 October, pilots handed over their surviving *Friedrichs* to other units and retired by road to Tobruk, where they boarded the flying-boats that were to take them to Italy. From here it was just a short hop across to San Pietro, in Sicily. But they would not be staying on the island for long.

While I. and III. *Gruppen* had been undertaking their forays into Russia and Egypt, Major Günther von Maltzahn's *Geschwaderstab*, together with II./JG 53, had remained in Sicily to continue operations, albeit on a much reduced scale, against Malta. But with no victorious ground forces beneath their wings, and no enemy reeling back in retreat before them, perhaps it is not surprising that the Sicily-based units did not enjoy the same levels of success as the other *Gruppen* during the latter part of 1942.

The 93 enemy aircraft claimed by II./JG 53 between May and October, for example, were only achieved at a cost of 15 of their own pilots lost in action. And the fact that all but seven of their victims were Spitfires is a telling indication of the improved state of Malta's defences by mid-1942 – no longer was the island's fate wholly dependent on a handful of war-weary Hurricanes.

Like the other *Gruppen*, however, II./JG 53 had its acknowledged *Experten*. Two pilots were alone responsible for over a third of all the victories. Oberleutnant Gerhard Michalski, the *Kapitän* of 4. *Staffel* (who would be appointed *Gruppenkommandeur* in August when Hauptmann Walter Spies was transferred to Russia to take command of I./JG 53), added 18 Allied aircraft to his score during this period, taking his total to 46. 5. *Staffel's* Oberfeldwebel Herbert Rollwage was not far behind with 16 – all Spitfires – but his overall score was still only 31. This meant that, whereas Gerhard Michalski would receive his Knight's Cross while still on Sicily (on 4 September for 40 kills, although his total was by then standing at 44), Herbert Rollwage would be required to add a further 22 victories to his tally before being similarly honoured in April 1944.

Eight of the twelve successes credited to the *Geschwaderstab* during this period in Sicily went to Leutnant Franz Schiess. The *Kommodore* himself claimed only one (his 64th), but 'Henri' von Maltzahn was being kept more than busy by the administrative side of his office, for he commanded not only his own II. *Gruppe* and 10.(*Jabo*) *Staffel* (prior to the latter's departure for Africa in August), but also the attached I./JG 77.

In addition, his area of responsibility often extended far beyond the well-worn confines of his units' operations against Malta. He had to organise and oversee temporary detachments to various other airfields throughout the eastern Mediterranean to help protect the Axis air and sea supply routes to NorthAfrica that were becoming increasingly vulnerable to the build-up of Allied strike forces in Egypt. On two occasions von Maltzahn was even obliged to rush elements of II. *Gruppe* to the El Alamein front for a few days to relieve the pressure on III./JG 53 at Quotaifiya.

A vine-leaf garlanded Oberfeldwebel Herbert Rollwage of 5./JG 53 clutches a cactus plant in a bomb tail 'vase' after returning to Comiso on 8 August 1942 upon the completion of his 300th mission. The rudder scoreboard tell its own story of future-*Experte* Rollwage's operational career to date – his first 12 victories (one of which was subsequently disallowed) against the Red Air Force, the remainder – starting with a Hurricane downed off the northwest tip of Malta on 4 January 1942 – gained over the RAF

Taken from the fourth machine, this photograph shows a *Schwarm* of early Bf 109G-2s from 5. *Staffel* on convoy escort duty (note the ventral long-range tanks) 'somewhere in the Mediterranean', circa September 1942

Between times *Stab* and II./JG 53 began exchanging their *Friedrichs* for new G-2s. Reinforced at the end of September by the arrival back from Russia of I./JG 53, flying a mix of G-2s and refurbished F-4s, von Maltzahn's units made ready to take part in one final Blitz against Malta.

It was launched on the morning of 11 October, but like all previous attempts to subjugate the island from the air – perhaps even more so given the revitalised state of the defences – it was doomed to failure. JG 53's performance illustrates the impossibility of the task. Although credited with 23 Spitfires in as many days' operations over and around Malta, it had, by the end of that time, suffered the loss of six of its own pilots.

Being picked over by RAF personnel in its rock and sandbagged blast pen – possibly at Bir El Abd, west of El Alamein – the wreckage of 4./JG 53's 'White 11' presents a sorry sight. This aircraft was one *Gustav* of Comiso-based II. *Gruppe* sent to North Africa to help reinforce III./JG 53 that would not be making it back across the Mediterranean to Sicily. It is not known whether the machine was destroyed by enemy action or blown up to prevent its falling into British hands, although the extent and type of damage suffered makes the latter seem the more likely

Geschwader-Adjutant Leutnant Franz Schiess is seen here in the cockpit of his G-2/trop at Comiso in September 1942. Schiess was by far the most successful pilot of JG 53's Stabsschwarm during the latter half of 1942, claiming 14 victories (taking him to 31 in all) against Kommodore von Maltzahn's three. Appointed Kapitän of 8. Staffel in February 1943, Schiess would be credited with a further 36 victories – and receive the Knight's Cross – before being killed in action on 2 September 1943

The Stab's Leutnant Franz Schiess had claimed the only success on the opening afternoon of the renewed onslaught, but this was offset by a pilot from II. Gruppe being reported missing. On 12 October, Leutnant Hans Roehrig of 3./JG 53, whose Knight's Cross had been announced ten days earlier at the time of I. Gruppe's return to Sicily from the eastern front, downed a pair of Spitfires to take his total to 60. On this date it was two NCO pilots of II./JG 53 who failed to return. And so it would go on until the end of the month.

I. Gruppe's sole casualty during this time was Unteroffizier Heinz Golinski, who was himself shot down immediately after claiming a Spitfire in a hectic dogfight south of Hal Far on 16 October. Having amassed his first 46 victories within the space of less than two months during I./JG 53's recent advance on Stalingrad, Heinz Golinski would be awarded a posthumous Knight's Cross on 30 December.

Any slim hopes the Axis may still have harboured of being able to overwhelm Malta's defending Spitfires were finally dashed on 29 October with the arrival of yet more carrier-borne reinforcements for the island. Major von Maltzahn received reinforcements of his own three days later when III./JG 53 touched down at San Pietro. Since being flown back to Italy from North Africa, the Gruppe had been hastily re-equipped with new G-4s. The net result of all this effort, however, was merely to allow Oberleutnant

Bore-sighting the guns of 4. Staffel's 'White 2'. This seemingly pristine Bf 109G-2/trop may be the replacement for the 'White 2' in which three-victory Leutnant Ewald Schumacher was reported missing off Malta on 11 October 1942

Franz Götz, the *Kapitän* of 9. *Staffel*, to claim a solitary Spitfire off the island of Gozo, Malta's smaller neighbour, on 1 November. It was the last success of the Malta battle for JG 53.

But there was now an entirely new threat in the offing. The Axis leaders were fully aware that large Allied troop convoys were converging on the western entrance to the Mediterranean. Fearing that their enemies might be preparing to invade Sardinia, III./JG 53 was hastily despatched to Elmas on that island's southern coast on 7 November.

**I./JG 53 prepares for its transfer to Tunisia early in November. 5. *Staffel* groundcrew sit among a jumble of personal baggage and service equipment as they wait to board the Ju 52/3ms that are to transport them across the Sicilian Narrows to North Africa . . .**

**. . . while 6. *Staffel*'s 'Yellow 9' and 'Yellow 5' wait equally patiently, their cockpits shrouded against the heat of the sun. Note the black triangle unit marking, outlined in white, on the tailfins of the Ju 52/3m transports in both shots**

Twenty-four hours later more than 100,000 American and British troops began to storm ashore on the beaches of Morocco and Algeria. The landings made clear the Allies' real intention – to destroy all Axis forces in North Africa by simultaneous advances from west and east. The German response was swift. Hitler ordered an immediate build-up of forces in Vichy French-held Tunisia. Among the first to be sent there were the fighters of JG 53 – von Maltzahn's *Stab*, plus II. and III. *Gruppen*, flew in to Tunis on 9 November. The bulk of I./JG 53 followed two weeks later.

The move heralded the beginning of the end for the 'Ace of Spades'. That end was, admittedly, still a long way off, but for JG 53 the remaining months of the war were to be months of successive withdrawals and retreats. It would be driven out of Tunisia, off Sicily, up through Italy, out of Normandy and from eastern Europe, before finally surrendering to American forces in Austria and southern Germany.

# THE MEDITERRANEAN, ACT II

I t was neither Stalingrad nor El Alamein, but Tunisia, that was to be the turning point in JG 53's war. When the *Geschwader* first arrived, the situation in North Africa was alarming but not yet critical. Its initial task was to safeguard the all-important sea and air supply routes across the Narrows from Sicily and Italy. In fact, the protection of these vital lifelines was to form the backdrop to JG 53's activities throughout the six-month campaign in Tunisia.

But as Allied forces began to close in on the Axis-held Tunisian bridgehead – the newly arrived 1st Army from Algeria to the west and the veterans of the 8th Army from across Libya to the east – von Maltzahn's pilots would be called upon to play an ever increasing part in the air and ground defence of Tunisia itself. To ease the operational burden, the *Kommodore* was also given temporary command of II./JG 51 and 11./JG 2 (the latter, a special high-altitude *Staffel*, was quickly incorporated into JG 53).

The 1st Army in neighbouring Algeria posed the greater threat. And it was here that JG 53 claimed its first success of the campaign – a single Spitfire brought down over the port of Bone on 12 November. Forty-eight hours later, the tables were turned when another encounter between 7. *Staffel* and Spitfires over Bone resulted in the loss of Leutnant Dietrich

Shortly after arriving in Tunisia, JG 53 assimilated Oberleutnant Julius Meimberg's specialised high-altitude 11./JG 2. Showing signs of a previous identity beneath its new individual number, 3. *Staffel*'s 'Yellow 8' – a pressurised G-1 – has almost certainly been taken over from 'Jule' Meimberg's *Staffel*

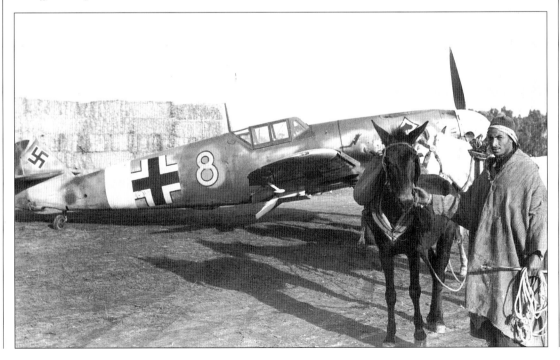

Hirsch. The following day, 15 November, the leading units of the 1st Army reached the Tunisian border. But for JG 53, a more ominous portent of things to come was the destruction of four of the *Stab*'s *Gustavs* on the ground at Tunis-el-Aouina during an Allied bombing raid.

By 17 November the 1st Army spearheads were only some 30 miles from Tunis itself. Given the speed of the Allies' advance, it was perhaps unwise to move III. *Gruppe* forward from Tunis to Djedeida on 21 November, where it was joined by most of I./JG 53, flying in from a brief deployment to Libya four days later. Both *Gruppen* had recently undergone a change of command. Hauptmann Friedrich-Karl 'Tutti' Müller, erstwhile *Staffelkapitän* of 1./JG 53, had replaced Hauptmann Walter Spies at the head of I. *Gruppe* upon the latter's transfer to III./JG 1, and Hauptmann Franz Götz, hitherto of 9. *Staffel*, had taken over III./JG 53 from the departing Major Erich Gerlitz.

The two new *Kommandeure* very nearly had their commands shot out from under them almost before they had time to settle in. On 25 November (some sources put it a day later), 17 American tanks suddenly appeared at Djedeida. Opening fire at a range of 875 yards, they first circled the field, probing its anti-tank defences. Finding none, they promptly mounted a cavalry charge across it, shooting at everything in their path. Luckily, those fighters not already aloft managed to get away in a mad, free-for-all scramble.

Unable to escape in time, the Stukas of II./StG 3 were not so fortunate. The unit lost an estimated 15-24 machines, either shot full of holes or mangled beneath the tracks of the 28-ton Grant tanks. Two somewhat chastened *Jagdgruppen* retired from the immediate vicinity of the fighting front – I./JG 53 headed to Bizerta, on the coast, and III./JG 53 returned to Tunis.

Up until this time all but three of the *Geschwader*'s 16 claims had been for Spitfires. But on 28 November, I. and II. *Gruppen* together accounted for five P-38 Lightnings (plus another Spitfire). Then, on the last day of the month, Hauptmann Götz's III./JG 53 was ordered to return to Sicily. Based at Comiso and San Pietro, it would be fully stretched not only covering the Mediterranean convoys from their northern termini, but also defending the transport airfields and embarkation ports in southern Italy from Allied bombing raids, as well as escorting the occasional reconnaissance machine on hazardous sorties to the hornets' nest of Spitfires that was now Malta.

But not as fully stretched as the *Gruppen* remaining in Tunisia. On 3 December, I. and II./JG 53, accompanied by Oberleutnant Julius Meimberg's 11./JG 2, moved forward again, this time to Mateur. The Allies' headlong advance was by now losing momentum, however, and by year-end it would be bogged down entirely in the wintry mountains west of Bizerta and Tunis. In addition to their ongoing convoy protection duties, the

These *Gustavs* of 7./JG 53 – the one in the foreground yet to have its 'Ace of Spades' badge applied – wear a somewhat unusual mottled camouflage. The presence of long-range tanks would suggest that this photo was taken in Sicily shortly after III. *Gruppe*'s return to the island at the beginning of December 1942

Tunisian-based units now began a punishing regime of escort missions for the bombers and dive-bombers attacking Allied positions, as well as flying ground-attack sorties in support of Axis troop movements and *freie Jagd* patrols in defence of their own airspace.

On 4 December they had their most successful day of the campaign to date when they were scrambled to intercept a formation of Bisleys (which they mistakenly identified as Douglas Bostons) passing close by Mateur. They were credited with the destruction of all 12 of the unescorted British bombers, including a trio for 'Jule' Meimberg. Among the other claimants were two members of 4./JG 53. One was *Staffelkapitän* Leutnant Fritz Dinger, whose P-38 earlier in the day had taken him to his half-century. To this he then added a brace of Bisleys. The other was Oberfeldwebel Stefan Litjens, who had lost an eye in Russia back in September 1941 and had only recently returned to the *Staffel* after a long convalescence. He claimed one of the bombers, plus a Spitfire in the same area to the southwest of Mateur a few minutes later.

The final tally for that 4 December was 18 aircraft destroyed. According to (the admittedly incomplete) *Geschwader* records, it was a total that JG 53 would never again be able to equal throughout the remaining months of the war.

The major reason for their declining success rate was the inexorable growth in Allied air power. On 18 December the now Oberstleutnant Günther von Maltzahn claimed the *Geschwader*'s first B-17 – one of a force of nearly 40 heavy bombers carrying out a raid on Bizerta harbour. The US four-engined bombers were to prove a new and formidable foe. Added to this, the imminent arrival of the improved Spitfire IX in the Mediterranean theatre, and the advent of the incomparable P-51, first encountered over Italy in the coming late summer, would all serve to put JG 53 just as much on the defensive in the air as the army units by then retreating on the ground below.

For the moment, though, von Maltzahn's pilots still felt that they were holding their own. On 23 December Fritz Dinger was awarded the Knight's Cross (officially for 49 victories, although his total on that date had already reached 53). The real stars in JG 53's firmament, however, were still the I. *Gruppe* triumvirate of Wilhelm Crinius, Friedrich-Karl

**Wearing the Knight's Cross awarded on 23 December 1942 (officially for 49 victories), 4./JG 53's *Staffelkapitän*, the now Oberleutnant Fritz Dinger, poses in front of his rudder scoreboard, which is already displaying 53 kills – the last, a B-25 of the American 310th Bomb Group shot down during an attack on Bizerta's Sidi Ahmed airfield on 5 December**

**'Yellow 6' of 6./JG 53, propeller blades bent and port undercarriage leg collapsed, finds itself in a rather undignified position after a taxiing accident, possibly at Bizerta, late in 1942. The cause of the mishap was reportedly faulty servicing**

Unlike the machines seen on page 86, these Bf 109G-4/trops of 8. *Staffel*, despite being pictured back on Sicily early in 1943, are still wearing an unmodified – albeit somewhat tatty – desert tan camouflage finish. The *Gustav* in the foreground, 'Black 1', is the mount of the *Staffelkapitän*, Oberleutnant Franz Schiess (see colour profile 24)

Müller and Wolfgang Tonne, whose scores at year-end were standing at 107, 103 and 102 respectively.

But not even such stellar individuals as these could affect the overall progress of the ground campaign. On 23 January 1943 the 'Desert Rats' of the 8th Army entered Tripoli, only some 100 miles from Libya's border with southern Tunisia. And by then the 114-victory Leutnant Wilhelm Crinius had already been ten days in Allied captivity, shot down by a US-flown Spitfire during a fighter-bomber escort mission to Bone harbour.

Despite a high level of operational activity, the closing week of January resulted in few successes – although the last day of the month did provide 'Tutti' Müller with a B-17 and a P-38, which took his total to 106. A spell of bad weather throughout much of the first half of February reduced the number of sorties flown by JG 53. It was during this period that the Germans counter-attacked through the Kasserine Pass, driving US troops back out of the wide valley that they had occupied only days earlier. It was the first time that the Allies had been forced to retreat since Gen Montgomery had fallen back on El Alamein. But Rommel could not sustain even this limited offensive, and by 25 February the Americans had regained all the ground that had been temporarily lost.

For the next month, despite rarely having more than 50 *Gustavs* serviceable at any one time, the pilots of JG 53 continued to exact a small but steady toll of Allied fighters – ten Spitfires and eleven P-38s in all – as they sought to carry out the heavy and varied operational demands still being made upon them. In March convoy protection duties assumed an even greater importance for the whole *Geschwader*, including III. *Gruppe* in Sicily, as the Axis powers poured yet more troops into Tunisia in preparation for the coming showdown in North Africa.

As Allied air superiority began to make itself felt, camouflage while on the ground became ever more important. Being refuelled here under all the netting at La Marsa, in Tunisia, in late February 1943 is 4. *Staffel's* 'White 2'

For a showdown there was undoubtedly going to be. On 21 March the 8th Army launched its assault on the Mareth Line. These were the frontier defences that guarded the Gabes Gap, the gateway into southern Tunisia. Within a week the British had punched their way through. For the next ten days the campaign in Tunisia was, in effect, a two-front war, with separate northern and southern sectors. But on 7 April the 1st and 8th Armies were to link up and begin pushing Axis troops into a shrinking perimeter in the northeastern tip of the country – an area that was soon being referred to as the 'Tunis bridgehead'.

Oberstleutnant von Maltzahn had divided his units (which had hitherto been operating almost exclusively on the northern front against the 1st Army) and sent part of Major Michalski's II. *Gruppe* to the southern sector, while the 8th Army was still battering at the Mareth defences. But when the *Kommodore* himself visited the Gabes area shortly afterwards, it was immediately apparent to him that Tunisia could not be held. Rightly fearing another Stalingrad, and not wishing to have his *Geschwader* needlessly sacrificed to a 'hold at all costs' order from on high, 'Henri' Maltzahn quietly began to send detachments of non-essential personnel back to the relative safety of Sicily. The first draft left even before the Mareth Line had been breached.

Hauptmann Franz Götz's III. *Gruppe* had, of course, been based in Sicily for the past three months, where it was fully engaged in convoy escort duties and the defence of the island from Allied bombing raids and roving fighter sweeps. Since the previous year, the boot had been transferred very firmly to the other foot, as Malta-based Spitfires were now appearing over Sicily in ever-increasing numbers. Despite this the *Gruppe*'s successes had been few. They included less than a dozen Spitfires and just two B-17s, the latter both claimed during a raid on Palermo on 22 March. Then, on 1 April, III./JG 53's strength was divided.

While the *Gruppenstab* and 7. *Staffel* remained on Sicily, 8./JG 53 was transferred to Tindja, in Tunisia, and 9./JG 53 sent to Sardinia, Italy's

Also pictured at II./JG 53's La Marsa base, but this time in March 1943, *Gruppenkommandeur* Hauptmann Gerhard Michalski (to right of rudder) listens to what Feldwebel Otto Russ (far left) has to say. This scene appears to have a slightly inquisitorial air about it – Fritz Dinger (in front of tailplane) certainly seems to be hanging on Russ' every word

An *Alarmstart* (emergency scramble) being acted out by pilots of 4./JG 53 at La Marsa in March 1943, in all probability for the benefit of an official war photographer. 'White 4' is the aircraft of *Staffelkapitän* Oberleutnant Fritz Dinger and 'White 5' that of Oberfeldwebel Stefan Litjens

second largest island, which was only some 120 miles north of Bizerta, and already receiving the attention of Allied bombers.

But it was in Tunisia that the land battle was raging, and where the end was now little more than a month away. On 2 April I. *Gruppe* had retired from Bizerta to Protville, north of Tunis. Three days later, Allied air forces began the systematic destruction of Axis lines of communication. The Luftwaffe responded as best it could, but the Stuka and fighter-bomber attacks that were mounted were small-scale and costly, not least to their escorting fighters. In March JG 53 had lost seven pilots in action. April's total would be exactly three times that figure.

The third week of the month witnessed an unaccustomed, albeit very brief, run of successes. The eighteenth of April's first victory was another B-17 brought down over Palermo by 7. *Staffel*. Then the action shifted to the coast of Tunisia. Late that afternoon, a large formation of Ju 52/3m

A group of pilots outside II./JG 53's camouflaged ops bunker at La Marsa. They are, from left to right, Feldwebel Otto Russ, *Gruppenkommandeur* Hauptmann Michalski, Oberleutnant Fritz Dinger, Leutnant Wolfgang Dreifke and Feldwebel Hans Feyerlein. Of these five, only two would survive the war. Dinger was to lose his life in a US bombing raid on Italy in September 1943, Feyerlein was killed in Defence of the Reich operations in March 1944 and Russ shot down over the Normandy invasion front in July 1944

Local labourers make good
bomb damage at La Marsa
while work continues on the
G-4/trop behind them

transports made another highly dangerous supply run to Tunis. After being hastily unloaded, they quickly took off again. Hugging the wave tops, the lumbering transports had hardly cleared Cape Bon (the north-eastern tip of Tunisia) before they were set upon by Allied fighters.

One *Staffel* of JG 53 was already flying as part of the Ju 52/3ms' mixed escort. Others rushed to the scene, and between them they claimed seven P-40s destroyed (for the loss of one of their own number). The *Geschwader's* final tally for the day was ten. But 18 April 1943 would go down in popular aviation history for the slaughter of the hapless transports, the 'Palm Sunday Massacre' resulting in 24 Junkers being shot down and a further 35 damaged.

The next day JG 53 went one better with 11 victories, the majority of them Spitfires (including a brace for Hauptmann Gerhard Michalski, the *Kommandeur* of II. *Gruppe*) that were providing cover for medium bombers carrying out a series of attacks on Luftwaffe airfields. Twenty-four hours later Michalski's *Gruppe* themselves felt the full weight of Allied air power when 12 of its *Gustavs* – the majority of them new G-6s – were written off or damaged in a bombing raid on the unit's La Marsa base.

On that 20 April 1943, the *Geschwader* was able to claim only six kills, all of which were credited to I./JG 53. But the day was overshadowed by the loss of Hauptmann Wolfgang Tonne. After accounting for three Spitfires (victories 120-122), the *Kapitän* of 3. *Staffel* returned to Protville and prepared to make his usual flamboyant 'sideslip' landing. On this occasion, however, he must have misjudged his height for some unknown reason. His 'Yellow 1' crashed near the edge of the field and immediately burst into flames.

The death of Wolfgang Tonne meant that the *Geschwader* now had only one centurion within its ranks – Hauptmann Friedrich-Karl Müller, the *Kommandeur* of I./JG 53. And it was 'Tutti' Müller's 115th victory (one of

122-victory Hauptmann Wolfgang
Tonne, *Staffelkapitän* of 3./JG 53,
was killed in a landing accident
at Protville on 20 April 1943

A day in the life of 5. *Staffel* back at Comiso, on Sicily, in early May 1943. While the *Gustavs* rest from the rigours of the recent Tunisian campaign in their rudimentary, camouflaged pens . . .

. . . the pilots amuse themselves as best they can. Here, they appear to be busy fixing up some kind of aerial – or could it perhaps be a washing line?

a trio of P-40s claimed on 30 April) that marked the 'official' end of I. *Gruppe*'s part in the Tunisian campaign. Handing its remaining machines over to II./JG 53 at La Marsa, the *Gruppe* was duly transferred to Sicily. Oberstleutnant von Maltzahn's *Geschwaderstab* also departed Tunisia for Comiso at this time.

II./JG 53 would hold out for another week, during which period it was joined for a while by elements of III. *Gruppe* flying in from Sicily and Sardinia. The *Geschwader*'s final days in Tunisia were anything but clear-cut. Several more missions were mounted from Sicily, either as part of the still ongoing supply and evacuation flights, or with the specific purpose of carrying out ground support operations over the fighting fronts in Tunisia. But with the loss of both Bizerta and Tunis on 7 May, the end was clearly at hand.

From their landing grounds on the Cape Bon peninsula, JG 53's pilots utilised the last hours of their African campaign shuttling back and forth between Tunisia and Sicily with a member of the ground staff stowed uncomfortably, but uncomplaining, in the rear fuselage of each *Gustav*. Among the last to leave were Oberstleutnant von Maltzahn and the machines of his *Geschwaderstab*, especially flown back in from Sicily to complete the process surreptitiously begun six weeks earlier – the extrication of JG 53's personnel from almost certain captivity. When Generaloberst von Arnim surrendered Tunisia on 12 May, some quarter of a million German and Italian troops were not so fortunate.

The *Geschwader* lost 75 pilots during the Tunisian campaign, the last shot down by P-40s off Cape Bon on 8 May. And although it had claimed nearly 300 victories in the same period, JG 53 had had 159 of its own machines destroyed or written off, with almost as many again damaged.

If Tunisia had tipped the scales of war against the unit, putting the 'Ace of Spades' for the first time firmly on the defensive, the coming weeks in Sicily – the 'stepping stone to mainland Europe' – were to bring home to the *Geschwader* the grim reality of their opponents' unassailable air superiority.

Once back in Sicily, with the *Geschwaderstab* and II. *Gruppe* taking up residence at Comiso, I. *Gruppe*, based at Catania, and III. *Gruppe*, remaining at Sciacca (the field on the island's southwest coast that it had occupied throughout much of the recent Tunisian campaign), *Kommodore* Oberstleutnant von Maltzahn tried to make good the material losses suffered in Africa. At the same time, he prepared the fresh intakes of new and inexperienced pilots for the next round of the battle against the Allied air forces.

He was not given much time, for on 21 May a formation of B-17s bombed Sciacca, destroying or damaging seven of III./JG 53's *Gustavs*. The Luftwaffe, which had begun every *Blitzkrieg* campaign of the early war years by attempting to destroy its opponent's air force on the ground, was about to get a taste of its own medicine. On 26 May the Allies launched a systematic bombing offensive specifically aimed at knocking out the Axis fighter airfields on Sicily.

Henceforth, not to mention the difficulties and dangers inherent in their normal escort duties – shepherding fighter-bombers and reconnaissance machines to Malta, and transports to the many outlying fields in the central Mediterranean – and the defence of the many military targets in Sicily and southern Italy, von Maltzahn's units would be hard pressed even to protect their own bases.

Such scenes of domestic bliss were soon to be shattered by the escalating Allied bombing offensive. The *Werk-Nummern* plastered all over this new G-6 reveal it to be 5. *Staffel*'s 'Black 6', which was damaged while taking off from Comiso on 26 May. It had presumably not yet been repaired when an Allied raid – possibly that by US B-24s on 17 June which put the field out of commission – reduced it to this sad state

For despite their occasional successes against four-engined bombers over Tunisia and Sicily, the *Geschwader* had never really found an effective counter to the US 'heavies'. The fighter pilots' perceived lack of success resulted in an order that two *Staffeln* were to be refitted as 'bomber *Staffeln*'. This entailed their being equipped with ventral bomb racks and required them to climb above the enemy formations and, once directly overhead, release a 250-kg bomb into the middle of them!

It was a technique that had been pioneered by *Jagdgruppe* in northern Germany a few weeks earlier (see *Osprey Aircraft of the Aces 29 - Bf 109F/G/K Aces of the Western Front* for further details). But it had not been particularly successful over the German Bight, and would prove even less so over the Mediterranean, not least because – unlike the early missions against the Reich by the not yet so 'Mighty Eighth' – the bombers targeting Sicily invariably enjoyed the benefit of fighter support. It is not known whether 5. or 8./JG 53 ever brought down a four-engined 'heavy' by dropping a bomb on it from above. However, on one occasion *Gustavs* of the former *Staffel* are reported to have jettisoned their bombs, unfortunately when some 3000 metres directly above their own Comiso base, and gone after a fleeing B-24 with their cannon alone!

Something had to be done about the US bombers, however. And that something was to relieve the local area *Jafü*, or fighter commander – who happened to be the affable and well-liked World War 1 ace, Generalmajor 'Onkel Theo' Osterkamp – and entrust the aerial defence of Sicily instead to the decidedly less avuncular *General der Jagdflieger* Adolf Galland. High Command was of the opinion that the Sicilian *Jagdgruppen* had not yet shaken off the effects of their recent experiences in Tunisia, and it was felt that Galland would be the man to restore their self-confidence and install a greater spirit of aggression into them. But his appointment would only lead to further problems.

In the meantime, the Allies were increasing their pressure. By mid-June they had taken the four small Italian-held islands that lay widely scattered approximately midway between the coast of Tunisia and Sicily. For a good week JG 53's activities were centred over the largest and northernmost of these islands, Pantelleria. Initially, it flew *freie Jagd* patrols trying to keep Allied bombers at bay, but to no avail, for on 11 June Pantelleria became the first island in history to surrender to aerial bombardment alone, displaying the white flag even before the first British troops set foot ashore. Thereafter, the *Geschwader* carried out a number of ultimately fruitless fighter-bomber escort sorties against the island's new occupants.

It was not just the offshore islands that the Allies were concentrating upon. On 15 June III. *Gruppe* reported another six *Gustavs* destroyed or damaged on the ground at Sciacca. And 48 hours later it was the turn of II./JG 53 at Comiso when seven of its fighters suffered the same fate. But on 21 June there was cause for celebration at both fields when the one-eyed Oberfeldwebel 'Steff' Litjens of 4. *Staffel* and Oberleutnant Franz Schiess – the *Kommodore*'s long-time wingman in the *Geschwaderstab*, but now the *Staffelkapitän* of 8./JG 53 – each received the Knight's Cross.

By this time, some six weeks after their return to Sicily, von Maltzahn's pilots had been credited with more than 50 Allied aircraft destroyed. The vast majority of these were still fighters, however, with only a handful each of twin-engined and four-engined bombers. And it was the bombers, of course, that were inflicting the damage. With the capture of the four small islands in the narrows, and the sea lanes to Sicily thus free of all obstacles, the Allies now began the task of isolating Sicily from mainland Italy by attacking the ports and ferry traffic in the Straits of Messina that separated the two.

This gave Adolf Galland the chance to launch his 'Big Blow'. His plan (which he would resurrect the following year in defence of the Reich) was to put every available fighter into the air to deliver a crushing, and hopefully decisive, blow against the enemy's bomber forces. His opportunity came on 25 June when the Americans mounted their heaviest single raid of the month against the port of Messina itself.

Although Messina lay within JG 53's area of operations (Maltzahn's *Geschwader* was responsible for the defence of the southern and eastern parts of Sicily, and JG 77 the western sector), Galland ordered both units to take-off – a force of some 80 fighters in all.

The mission turned into a shambles. Firstly, the *Jagdgruppen* were unable to maintain formation in the poor visibility and became strung out. Then the Axis monitoring posts lost track of the bombers. It was not until their own fuel was running dangerously low that the leading *Gustavs* eventually spotted a group of B-17s low over the water nearly 100 miles off the northwest tip of Sicily, running hard for Africa. The 80 fighters reportedly achieved just five victories between them.

That same evening a telex was received from an enraged Hermann Göring, Commander-in-Chief of the Luftwaffe, demanding that every *Jagdgruppe* that had taken part in the operation was to put forward one pilot who was to be court-martialled for 'cowardice in the face of the enemy'. Although the courts were convened few, if any, of those accused were sentenced. But the affair did little to lift morale. Nor did the Reichsmarschall's order of a few days later, which decreed that every *Schwarm* (flight of four aircraft) that took off on a mission was to return either with at least one kill, or with every one of its fighters damaged as proof that they had engaged in combat with the enemy. Otherwise, court-martials were again threatened. Oberstleutnant von Maltzahn confessed to being ashamed at having to read such an order to his assembled pilots.

The latter may therefore be forgiven if they were not in the best of spirits when, on 3 July, the Allies began the final week's softening-up prior to invading Sicily. Yet the days that followed were to prove the most successful of the *Geschwader*'s entire three months on the island. Unfortunately, they also witnessed the highest casualties, including four of von Maltzahn's nine *Staffelkapitäne* – the very people he could least afford to lose.

The first to die was Leutnant Herbert Broennle, the recently appointed *Kapitän* of 2. *Staffel*. Already wearing the Knight's Cross for his 57 victories while serving with JG 54 on the eastern front (where he had also been severely wounded), Broennle had achieved just one further kill – a B-24 – since taking command of 2./JG 53. It was during a low-level dogfight with Spitfires south of Catania on 4 July that his 'Black 8' was hit and dived vertically into the ground from a height of less than 1000 ft.

Against the loss of Herbert Broennle, plus two other pilots wounded, JG 53 had, however, claimed nine Allied aircraft destroyed during the course of that 4 June. It was the *Geschwader*'s most successful day over Sicily to date. The same number would be credited to its pilots 24 hours later – and this time the total included six B-17s.

Leutnant Herbert Broennle had been *Kapitän* of 2. *Staffel* for less than a fortnight, and had achieved only one victory with JG 53, when he was killed in action against Spitfires on 4 July 1943 . . .

. . . and just nine days later *Kommodore* von Maltzahn lost another of his *Staffelkapitäne* to Spitfires when 75-victory Hauptmann Hans Roehrig of 9./JG 53 (seen here as a leutnant upon being awarded the Knight's Cross in October 1942) was reported missing over the Straits of Messina

The fifth of June was a day of widespread raids by American 'heavies' and medium bombers on airfields and other military targets across the length and breadth of Sicily. But it was the Flying Fortresses attacking the airfield complex to the west of Catania that reportedly took the full brunt of another of Galland's 'Big Blows' – an estimated 100 fighters from both JG 53 and 77. Each *Geschwader* was credited with downing six Boeing bombers, but the US group that came under attack admitted the loss of just three!

JG 53's *Gustavs* also became embroiled with the bombers' escorting fighters. And although one Spitfire provided Hauptmann Friedrich-Karl Müller with the last victory he would claim while with the *Geschwader* (Nos 117 or 118 according to conflicting sources), another group of 35-40 Spitfires pounced upon Oberleutnant Willi Klein, the *Kapitän* of 1. *Staffel*, and his wingman. Both were shot down into the sea somewhere off Cape Passero (the southeastern tip of Sicily).

Oberstleutnant von Maltzahn's pilots were able to claim eight victories on each of two other consecutive days, 8 and 9 July, without loss to themselves. Then, before daybreak on 10 July, the first Allied troops stormed ashore from more than 2000 vessels and landing craft lying off a 90-mile stretch of the Sicilian coast between Licata and Syracuse.

Over the next 12 hours, from eight in the morning until eight in the evening, JG 53 flew at least nine separate missions – reconnaissance, *freie Jagd* and fighter-bomber escort – during which time it was credited with 17 victories (over half of them Spitfires) at the expense of two 5. *Staffel* NCOs wounded. The following day saw a marked reduction in their number of successes. But among the six fighters (and one B-26 Marauder) claimed, a pair of P-38s enabled Oberleutnant Hans Roehrig – the *Staffelkapitän* of 9./JG 53, and the *Geschwader*'s second-highest scorer after 'Tutti' Müller – to boost his tally to 75.

But the *Geschwader*'s performance failed to satisfy a by-now thoroughly rattled Hermann Göring, who fired off another telex on the evening of 11 July;

'Together with the fighter pilots in France, Norway and Russia, I look with scorn upon the pilots in the south. I want to see an immediate improvement, and expect all pilots to display more fighting spirit. Should this improvement not be forthcoming, all pilots – from *Kommodores* downwards – must expect to be reduced to the rank of aircraftman and sent to serve as infantry on the eastern front.'

But to those facing the daily reality of overwhelming enemy superiority in the air, and constant bombardment on the ground, the Reichs-marschall's empty and increasingly irrational threats now counted for little. For by this time the *Geschwader* was already preparing to evacuate its damaged, but still airworthy, *Gustavs* across the Straits of Messina to mainland Italy, while most of Major Michalski's II./JG 53 was withdrawn from Sicily altogether and sent northwards for hurried re-equipment with a new complement of G-6s.

On 13 July Oberleutnant Hans Roehrig was lost in action against Spitfires south of Catania. And after four unserviceable machines of 9. *Staffel* were blown up at Torrazzo (both II. and III. *Gruppen* had retired from the coastal regions to landing grounds in the Gerbini complex west of Catania during the latter half of June), the rest of III./JG 53 flew out to

Lecce, on the heel of Italy. Two days later four of II. *Gruppe*'s fighters that had been left behind at Rammacca were likewise destroyed to deny them to the advancing enemy.

The end of JG 53's part in the Sicilian campaign was approaching rapidly. But, like the final days in Tunisia, it was by no means a straightforward process. For the past month I./JG 53 had been shuttling back and forth between fields in Sicily and across the straits in southern Italy. Fate finally caught up with 'Tutti' Müller's *Gruppe* at Vibo Valentia, an airfield on the toe of Italy north of the Straits of Messina, where it was attacked by a force of 100+ medium bombers on 16 July. No fewer than 21 of the unit's fighters were blown up or written off. I./JG 53 would be out of action for the best part of the next three weeks.

More than 80 fighters had been destroyed in the raid (other *Jagdgruppen*, including I./JG 77, were currently sharing Vibo Valentia), and vehicles, hangars and fuel dumps were all left in flames. Adolf Galland's HQ also happened to be located at Vibo. It is reported that, as soon as the bombers had passed, the *General der Jagdflieger* climbed into his car and headed for Naples 'to find out what was going on'. He presumably didn't like what he heard. For not long afterwards the poisoned chalice of southern area defence was back in the hands of 'Onkel Theo' Osterkamp.

With I. *Gruppe* non-operational and III. *Gruppe* scattered on fields across southern Italy, it fell to the newly returned and re-equipped II./JG 53 to carry out the *Geschwader*'s final operations over Sicily. Initially flying from bases in the Lecce region, Major Michalski's *Gruppe* mounted a series of mainly *freie Jagd* sweeps, nearly every one of which resulted in contact with the Allied fighters that were now already occupying Comiso and other ex-Luftwaffe airfields in the southern part of the island.

**The end of the line at Comiso. A pair of apparently intact G-6/trops abandoned by II./JG 53 attract the attention of two RAF officers. The spiral-spinnered machine on the left carries the chevron insignia (just visible above the wing leading edge) of a *Stab* aircraft, while the 'gunboat' on the right belonged, until recently, to 6. *Staffel*. Note the dismembered remains of a scribble-camouflaged Ju 88 bomber lying in the foreground**

These encounters appear to have been mostly inconclusive, however. In the ten days leading up to 26 July, II./JG 53 suffered just one combat casualty (a 4. *Staffel* pilot killed in action against B-17s over the Gulf of Taranto on the 23rd) and was credited with only five victories – two fighters and a trio of B-26 Marauders (the latter all on the 24th).

Then on 27 July, having transferred in the meantime to Scalea (a landing ground on the west coast of Italy approximately mid-way between Vibo Valentia and Naples), II. *Gruppe* had nine of its *Gustavs* destroyed or damaged in a raid by a mixed force of B-25 and B-26 medium bombers. More seriously, the *Geschwader* lost its fourth *Staffelkapitän* in the space of a month. Oberleutnant Fritz Dinger, the *Kapitän* of 4./JG 53, had claimed his 67th victim (a P-40) while leading a *Schwarm* over Sicily earlier that same morning. Returning to Scalea, the four machines were still being refuelled and re-armed for their next mission when the first wave of USAAF bombers struck. Fritz Dinger was the only casualty, killed in his slit trench by a bomb splinter.

JG 53 were little involved in the final two weeks of the Sicilian campaign. By early August – with I. *Gruppe* at San Severo (part of the Foggia airfield complex close to the Italian Adriatic coast) still making good its recent losses – II. and III./JG 53 had taken up residence on two landing grounds to the north and east of Naples.

It was Hauptmann Franz Götz's III. *Gruppe* which was responsible for the *Geschwader*'s first significant success over mainland Italy, being credited with six B-24s downed during a raid on Foggia on 16 August. Seventy-two hours later, elements of all three *Gruppen* were in action against strong formations of B-17s and B-24s returning to the same target. Ten 'heavies' (and a single P-38) were claimed, but this time there was a price to pay – one pilot killed and at least two wounded.

Despite this fairly auspicious start, it would be the end of the year before JG 53 was able to repeat this kind of performance against the US 'heavies'. For much of their time in Italy, the *Geschwader*'s pilots were employed in more tactical roles. And the majority of their opponents – and victims – were either fighters or medium bombers. Here, too, they got off to a good start, accounting for 14 P-38s in a huge dogfight over the coast near Naples on 20 August (the Lightnings, for their part, claimed 13 Axis fighters destroyed and many others damaged). During the course of the next two days, II. and III. *Gruppen* were then credited with 18 Marauders downed while attacking marshalling yards in the Naples area. And on 30 August they added a further 11 P-38s to their collective scores for the loss of one 4. *Staffel* pilot.

But the weight of Allied numbers continued to make itself felt. On 26 August Major Michalski's II. *Gruppe* had 11 of its *Gustavs* destroyed or damaged during a raid by medium bombers on their field at Cancello near Naples. JG 53 were to suffer many such attacks on their Italian bases, losing a total of almost 80 fighters – well over 50 per cent of their official complement – to bombing and strafing before the *Geschwader*'s final withdrawal from the country.

In the air, losses were also starting to rise steadily, and this inevitably led to a corresponding fall in the number of victories achieved. August's high rate of success could not be maintained, with September seeing just 18 enemy aircraft brought down. And never again in Italy would the *Geschwader*'s collective daily total reach double figures.

Oberst Günther *Freiherr* von Maltzahn pictured shortly before relinquishing command of JG 53, the *Geschwader* he had led for almost three years

'Henri' von Maltzahn's place was taken by Major Helmut Bennemann, who was posted in from JG 52 (note this aircraft's 'winged sword' badge) and would command the *Geschwader* until its final surrender

During this period the two main events were the Allied landings at Salerno and Anzio in September 1943 and January 1944 respectively. It was in the weeks leading up to, and during, these operations that JG 53 lost – in addition to dozens of younger and more inexperienced pilots – six more of its *Staffelkapitäne*.

The first was another of the *Geschwader*'s dwindling band of high scorers. Two of the Lightnings downed on 30 August had taken Franz Schiess' total to 67. On 2 September Hauptmann Schiess led his 8. *Staffel* into action against a large formation of B-26s that were attacking marshalling yards northeast of Naples as part of the softening-up process prior to the Salerno landing. Unable to penetrate the medium bombers' strong fighter screen, Schiess followed the enemy force back out over the Gulf of Salerno, only to be shot down himself by a pair of P-38s.

Two days later Oberleutnant Martin Laube, *Staffelkapitän* of 5./JG 53, was among those who took off from Cancello in response to the reported approach of US heavy bombers. In fact, the B-17s were forced to abort their mission against airfields in southern Italy due to the appalling conditions. And it is believed that these were also the cause of Laube's loss. He was posted missing after last being seen flying into a bad weather front. On 10 September, another *Staffelkapitän*, 2./JG 53's Oberleutnant Dietrich Kasten, would also be reported missing after disappearing during a routine transfer flight.

Italy had surrendered on 8 September, allowing Anglo-American forces to pour ashore almost unopposed at Salerno the following day. For the next week the *Geschwader* operated against the bridgehead, flying *freie Jagd* missions and escorting bombers, fighter-bombers and their own rocket-equipped *Gustavs* – newly delivered to II. *Gruppe* – in attacks on shipping and landing craft lying off the beaches. Casualties, and victories, remained minimal during these operations, but material damage was high, and made even higher by two heavy bombing raids on airfields in the Rome area to which JG 53 had only just retired. On 16 September 15 of II. *Gruppe*'s G-6s were destroyed or damaged at Littoria, and 24 hours later 14 of III./JG 53's machines suffered the same fate at Ciampino (where one pilot was killed and seven others wounded).

On that same 17 September, Allied troops pushing northwards from the toe of Italy linked up with the Salerno bridgehead, and there now began the painfully slow, but dogged, advance that would take the Allies up the length of Italy, across the Alps and into Austria.

By early October the Naples and Foggia airfields had been lost and Sardinia and Corsica evacuated. The following days and weeks would witness some fundamental changes within the *Geschwader*. The three *Gruppen* had undergone further withdrawals, with II. and III./JG 53 retiring to northern Italy for yet another round of re-equipment. This left just 'Tutti' Müller's I./JG 53 operational to the north of Rome.

On 3 October Oberst Günther von Maltzahn relinquished command of the *Geschwader* that he had led for just five days short of three years – the longest tenure of office of any wartime fighter *Kommodore*. Both Friedrich-Karl Müller and Major Kurt Ubben (of JG 77) would serve in acting capacities until the *Geschwader*'s sixth and final *Kommodore*, the 88-victory Major Helmut Bennemann, hitherto the *Gruppenkommandeur* of I./JG 52 on the eastern front, arrived to take command early in November.

A G-6/trop, complete with dust filter on the supercharger air intake and sun umbrella clamps below the windscreen, is serviced and refuelled between operations in central Italy in late 1943

It is ironic that 'Henri' von Maltzahn, who had been one of the targets of Göring's wrath and among the recipients of the Reichsmarschall's infamous telexes during the Sicilian campaign, should now be selected to replace Generalleutnant Theo Osterkamp as the new *Jafü Oberitalien*, or Fighter-leader Upper Italy!

Also, early in October II./JG 53 left Italy altogether. Passing its *Gustavs* over to I. *Gruppe*, the unit was flown north to Vienna-Seyring, where its pilots were to retrain as a dedicated anti-bomber unit. Their opponents remained the same – the US 'heavies' flying up from the Mediterranean. But henceforth II. *Gruppe* would be operating as part of the Defence of the Reich organisation. Its first mission on 2 November – which also happened to be the second mounted by the newly constituted Fifteenth Air Force – resulted in the claiming of four B-17s destroyed out of a mixed force raiding the Wiener Neustadt aircraft works. One of the four Flying Fortresses provided *Gruppenkommandeur* Major Gerhard Michalski with his 60th victory.

II./JG 53's next successes were not achieved until 7 January 1944. On this date it was credited with 15 P-38s downed during the course of a running dogfight that began at an altitude of 26,000 ft south of Wiener Neustadt and ended close to ground level in northern Yugoslavia. During the following five months – based first in Austria and then, from March 1944, on airfields in southwest Germany – the *Gruppe* would claim some 70 heavy bombers (and about a tenth that number of their escorting fighters). But the price paid was high. II./JG 53 lost more than 60 of its own pilots killed, missing or wounded. The Battle for the Reich was already turning into a straightforward war of attrition. Numbers counted. And in any such contest against the manpower and industrial might of the United States, there could only be one outcome.

Shortly after II./JG 53's retirement from Italy there was a division of labour between the two remaining *Gruppen*. While I./JG 53 continued to operate in a tactical role in support of the fighting fronts south of Rome, Major Franz Götz's III./JG 53 up at Reggio Emilia was to be converted into a 'heavy' *Jagdgruppe* – the Luftwaffe term that now denoted a specialised anti-bomber unit. Equipped with 'gunboats' armed with 20 or 30 mm cannon in underwing gondolas (and with 7. *Staffel* later being fitted with rocket launchers), it was to form part of the aerial defences of industrial northern Italy.

From its bases in the shadows of the Alps, the *Gruppen* would also, in effect, be providing the first line of defence against the 'heavies' of the Fifteenth Air Force that were soon to be reaching deeper into Austria and other parts of Hitler's southern territories. But like so many of the Luftwaffe's late war plans that looked good on paper, things did not always work out so neatly in practice. The units' roles were, more often than not, dictated by circumstances rather than by officialdom. And – until they were reversed altogether – III./JG 53 would continue to bring down both fighters and medium bombers, while I./JG 53 would be credited with a number of four-engined bombers destroyed.

Nevertheless, it was III. *Gruppe* who would claim two B-17s out of a force attacking marshalling yards at Bolzano on 11 November, and who, after a prolonged spell of bad weather, did even better on 28 December when it accounted for seven B-24s shot down during a raid on the yards at Vincenza. In fact, ten Liberators failed to return from this mission, the largest single loss to date suffered by the embryonic Fifteenth Air Force. It was also Hauptmann Jürgen Harder, the *Staffelkapitän* of 7./JG 53, who, on 5 December, had been awarded the *Geschwader*'s first Knight's Cross for six months – reportedly for 40 victories, although his actual total is believed still to have been one short of that figure at the time.

All this while the pilots of I. *Gruppe* had been at full stretch flying as many as three or four missions a day in support of 10. *Armee*'s defence of the Gothic Line running through the mountains south of Rome. It was in an attempt to break the deadlocked land campaign that the Allies landed at Anzio, behind the Gothic defences, but still some 30 miles short of the Italian capital, on 22 January 1944. And it was at this precise juncture that I. and III./JG 53 perforce exchanged roles.

The former's recent low-level operations over the coastal plains and in the mountains around Monte Cassino had resulted in many machines sustaining damage. The process was completed by two bombing raids on Centocelle airfield on 13 and 14 January, during which fragmentation bombs sieved every one of the *Gruppe*'s remaining *Gustavs*, leaving not a single machine serviceable. A week later, on the eve of the Anzio landings, I./JG 53 was withdrawn to Maniago, near Udine, in northeastern Italy.

In the meantime, III./JG 53 had been based at Villa Orba, also close to Udine, for the best part of a month. Further bad weather had curtailed its operations throughout the first half of January, and when its pilots finally went up again on the 16th against a force of B-17s attacking the aircraft components plant at Klagenfurt, in Austria, the results were far from satisfactory. Their sole claim was for one of the bombers' escorting P-38s, against which they lost four of their own pilots (one brought down in a mid-air collision with the stricken Lightning). The performance of the rocket-equipped Bf 109Gs of 7. *Staffel* was deemed to be particularly disappointing.

III./JG 53 *Gruppenkommandeur* Major Franz Götz clambers out of his G-6 'gunboat' back at Villa Orba, in northern Italy, in January 1944 after what has presumably been an abortive anti-bomber sortie – if he had made contact with the enemy, his first action would have been to jettison that unwieldy, oil-streaked drop tank

The withdrawal of I./JG 53 from the Rome sector just 24 hours prior to the Anzio landings had left an alarming gap in the southern front. The proximity of the Allied beachhead to the Italian capital was a threat that could not be ignored. And III. *Gruppe*, apparently serving little purpose in the far northeast, was ordered down to Orvieto, less than 60 miles north of Rome, on 24 January. Four days later, Franz Götz's pilots, specially trained to combat high-altitude heavy bombers, began flying ground-attack sorties against the Anzio beaches. Not surprisingly, their losses started to escalate rapidly.

But there were still victories to be had. On 7 February Hauptmann Jürgen Harder – whose 7. *Staffel* was now employing its rockets against the Anzio-Nettuno harbour installations and offshore shipping – scored the day's sole success. The Spitfire he shot off his wingman's tail took his score to 40. A week later Harder was appointed *Gruppenkommandeur* of I./JG 53 when 'Tutti' Müller departed to take over IV./JG 3 in Defence of the Reich. Hauptmann, later Major, Harder would remain in command of I. *Gruppe* until January 1945. His successor at the head of 7. *Staffel*, Oberleutnant Rolf Klippgen, lasted just four days before falling victim to a Spitfire on 19 February.

On 20 February III./JG 53 made the short hop from Orvieto to Arlena, some 25 miles to the southwest. But yet more bad weather would keep the *Gruppe* out of action until mid-March. When conditions finally eased, the third Battle of Cassino was already in progress. The ensuing days and weeks therefore saw much of their activity centred over the mountains rather than against the Anzio beachhead. It was during this period that 7. *Staffel*'s Leutnant Günther Seeger received the Knight's Cross. Awarded on 26 March for his 46 victories, Seeger had in fact reached this figure almost two months earlier by downing a B-26 on 29 January while still an oberfeldwebel.

By the end of April the pilots of III./JG 53 had added 15 more kills in all to their collective scoreboard. One, a P-47 claimed on the 14th, provided the half-century for Oberleutnant Franz Barten, who had been appointed *Kapitän* of 9. *Staffel* after the loss of Hans Roehrig over Sicily.

More worrying, however, was the fact that for the first time their own casualties exceeded the number of victories claimed. For in the same period the *Gruppe* had reported the loss of nine pilots killed, two captured and nine wounded.

To the north, meanwhile, I./JG 53 were adapting rather better to its new anti-bomber role. Not much action was seen at first, and so the early part of February at Maniago could be spent in training new pilots. Then, after a couple of false starts, the *Gruppe* achieved its first major success on 25 February when it brought down seven B-24s and a single B-17 during the Fifteenth Air Force's raid on Regensburg (this was the coordinated attack by both the Eighth and Fifteenth Air Forces that concluded the USAAF's 'Big Week' offensive against Germany's aircraft manufacturing plants (see *Osprey Aircraft of the Aces 68 - Bf 109 Defence of the Reich Aces* for further details).

On 18 March the Luftwaffe's own airfields in the Udine region were the targets for the Fifteenth Air Force's bombers. This time I./JG 53

Franz Götz takes off on another mission, this time over the Rome-Anzio region, sometime in the spring of 1944. Götz' three kills in this area during the first half of 1944 – a P-47 and two Spitfires – would take his score exactly to the half-century mark

8./JG 53's 'Black 16' – pilot unknown – prepares to take to the skies of central Italy in the late spring of 1944 as the battle for the Anzio bridgehead nears its end

The only loss suffered in the 25 April action against US Liberators, in which both *Geschwaderkommodore* Major Helmut Bennemann and I. *Gruppe*'s *Kommandeur* Hauptmann Jürgen Harder bailed out wounded, was that of Unteroffizier Rudolf Lehmann of 2./JG 53, who was shot down southeast of Bologna. Portrayed here as a gefreiter, Lehmann typifies the many young pilots who came and went through the ranks of JG 53 without scoring a single victory

was credited with six B-17s and a trio of P-47s. But unlike the earlier Regensburg raid, which had cost it just one pilot missing and one wounded, the defence of the unit's own bases came at a higher price – six killed or missing, plus four wounded. Two of those killed were lost in a dogfight with P-38s over Maniago itself.

Further casualties – some 20 in all – were suffered during the next month, by the end of which time I. *Gruppe*, together with the *Geschwaderstab*, had transferred from the Udine area down to Bologna. It was from here that they scrambled on 25 April when a formation of B-24s was reported approaching from the south. In an action lasting the best part of 40 minutes, they claimed eight of the Liberators. The first fell to Major Helmut Bennemann, taking the *Geschwaderkommodore*'s overall total to 90. And the second of Hauptmann Jürgen Harder's pair gave I./JG 53's *Kommandeur* his half-century. Both Bennemann and Harder had to bail out wounded, however, the former having been hit by return fire from the B-24s and the latter after colliding with (some accounts claim ramming) his second victim.

Against a scenic Alpine backdrop, Hauptmann Jürgen Harder (right) – seemingly recovered from his wounds – confers with Oberleutnant Erich Thomas, *Kapitän* of 2./JG 53, in front of one of the *Staffel*'s rocket-equipped *Gustavs* . . .

This was the *Gruppe*'s last significant confrontation with US 'heavies' over Italy. On 9 May I./JG 53 would be sent to Rumania to help defend that country's vital oil installations. It would not serve under Bennemann's command again.

*Stab* and III. *Gruppe* continued to fight on in Italy for a few weeks longer. Mid-May saw the launch of the fourth Battle of Cassino, which finally resulted in a link-up with the embattled Anzio bridgehead on the 25th. The following day, Major Franz Götz, the *Kommandeur* of III./JG 53, became the latest of the *Geschwader*'s semi-centurions when he downed the second of a pair of Spitfires. Then, after several more encounters with Spitfires close to the Italian capital, III. *Gruppe* was suddenly ordered back up to Maniago on 2 June. Here, it spent a good week readying pilots and aircraft for a resumption of anti-bomber operations. The first of these took place on 9 June, when three B-24s were claimed against the loss of an unteroffizier to the 'heavies' escorting P-38 Lightnings.

Five days later, III./JG 53 was credited with two more B-24s and a single P-47. Achieved at the cost of another two unteroffiziere killed in action, these would prove to be the last successes of the *Geschwader*'s long Mediterranean career. Before June was out the *Gruppe* had handed its remaining *Gustavs* to a unit of the National Republican Air Force – that part of Italy's air arm that had continued to fight on alongside Germany after the Italian surrender of September 1943. It had then departed by rail to the homeland for re-equipment and subsequent deployment in Defence of the Reich.

. . . before checking to see how work is progressing on his own 'gunboat' (note the port underwing cannon gondola lying on the ground at front right). Shortly after these shots were taken Hauptmann Harder's I. *Gruppe* was to leave northern Italy for Rumania

# END IN THE EAST AND WEST

The end of JG 53's lengthy involvement in the Mediterranean war, which had begun over Malta back in December 1941, also heralded, in essence, the end of the *Geschwader*'s history as a separate and individual entity. For most of the remaining months of hostilities, its component *Gruppen*, divided between eastern and western fronts, were but part of the larger infrastructures of the commands fighting the Luftwaffe's final major daylight campaigns of the war – those against the American and Soviet air forces soon to be roaming at will over the skies of the Reich itself.

And like every other unit locked in these unequal struggles, their story becomes a repetitive catalogue of declining successes and mounting casualties as the constant attrition they were suffering was time and again made good – at least numerically – by fresh intakes of ever younger and ever more inadequately trained replacements. Coupled to the growing shortage of aviation fuel, they were embarking upon a relentless downward spiral that would only be brought to a halt by Germany's surrender in May 1945.

The first *Gruppe* to experience the harsh reality of Defence of the Reich operations had been Major Gerhard Michalski's II./JG 53, which had been transferred from Italy to Vienna-Seyring in mid-October 1943. Initially, while still based in Austria and facing the fledgling Fifteenth Air Force flying up across the Alps from the Mediterranean, it had managed to hold its own. Indeed, its pilots were credited with some 40 US bombers and fighters destroyed against approximately half that number of their own killed, missing or wounded.

But when the unit moved to the Frankfurt area of western Germany at the beginning of March 1944, it found the more powerful and experienced Eighth Air Force a very different proposition indeed. Its first successes – a trio of B-17s downed north of Koblenz on 4 March – cost the *Gruppe* three dead and one wounded. A claimant for one of the Flying Fortresses, Oberfeldwebel Rudolf Ehrenberger, was himself killed in action during II./JG 53's next clash with the Eighth's 'heavies' northwest of Berlin four days later. The 49-victory Ehrenberger would be honoured with a posthumous Knight's Cross on 6 April.

Another oberfeldwebel – one already wearing the Knight's Cross – was also lost to the *Gruppe* in March. The one-eyed Stefan Litjens had just accounted for two B-17s near Brunswick on 23 March when the canopy of his own 'White 5' was damaged by fire from the bombers and flying splinters injured his remaining good eye. Although practically blinded, he was able to make an emergency belly landing. But 'Steff' Litjens' days of combat flying were finally over.

Exactly one month later, on 23 April, Major Gerhard Michalski was appointed *Kommodore* of JGz.b.V. (a special-purposes *Geschwaderstab* whose task was to coordinate the operations of five Defence of the Reich

*Jagdgruppen*, each drawn from a different *Geschwader*). Michalski's place at the head of II./JG 53 – one of the five units under his new overall command – was taken by Hauptmann Julius Meimberg, whose 11./JG 2 had been incorporated into JG 53 at the start of the Tunisian campaign.

The departure of Gerhard Michalski meant that II./JG 53's top scorer was now Oberfeldwebel Herbert Rollwage, who had received the Knight's Cross less than three weeks previously for his then total of 53. He would take this figure to 60 with a P-51 downed over eastern France on 27 May. Rollwage's victim was one of the first Mustang fighters to fall to JG 53 – it is believed that the one or two previous claims for P-51s over Italy had, in fact, been either F-6 reconnaissance or A-36 attack variants.

By this time the *Gruppe* had transferred from Frankfurt-Eschborn first to Biblis, close to the Rhine, and then to Öttingen, about 62 miles east-northeast of Stuttgart. It was from Öttingen on 30 May that II./JG 53 claimed a trio of Flying Fortresses from a force attacking aircraft plants in central Germany. The last of the three was victory 36 for 'Jule' Meimberg, its recently appointed *Gruppenkommandeur*.

Meimberg's kill was also the last of the 50+ US machines that II./JG 53 had downed since taking up residence at Frankfurt. But, indicative of their own escalating casualties, it had taken more than 40 pilots killed or wounded to achieve this result.

The skies above the Reich were unnaturally quiet for the next week as the Eighth Air Force turned its attention to targets in northern France, preparatory to the D-Day landings. The German High Command was aware that invasion was imminent, but uncertain as to exactly where along the French Channel coast the Allies were about to strike. Unlike the Panzer divisions in northwest Europe, however, which could only be moved with the express permission of the *Führer*, the Luftwaffe already had in place contingency plans to rush almost all of the Defence of the Reich fighter units to France the moment the first enemy troops set foot ashore.

II./JG 53's sealed orders, opened on the morning of 6 June 1944, instructed the *Gruppe* to proceed with all despatch, staging via Le Mans, to Vannes, on the French Biscay coast. But at Le Mans it got a foretaste of what lay ahead when two pilots were killed and four transport Ju 52/3ms carrying much of the *Gruppe*'s equipment were shot down by patrolling US fighters while coming in to land.

After arriving at Vannes on 7 June II./JG 53 managed nonetheless to mount a number of *freie Jagd* sweeps. But within a week, during which time it suffered two heavy bombing raids, the *Gruppe* was forced to seek less exposed accommodation. Its *Staffeln* were, in fact, next dispersed inland on three small landing grounds north of the River Loire. Here, although relatively safe from high-altitude bombing, they were at the mercy of the arguably even more dangerous hordes of low-level fighter-bombers on the lookout for the slightest sign of Luftwaffe activity on the ground.

In little more than another week, their nine(!) remaining serviceable *Gustavs* were therefore transferred out of harm's way to Champfleury, east of the Seine. II./JG 53 was now to be tasked with supporting German ground troops around the hotly contested area of Caen. And it was on 2 July, some six miles south-southeast of the town of Caen itself, that a Spitfire – possibly Canadian-flown – gave Oberleutnant Günther Seeger, the *Kapitän* of 4. *Staffel*, his half-century.

Seen here as a leutnant sporting the Knight's Cross awarded for 46 victories on 26 March 1944, Oberleutnant Günther Seeger was appointed *Staffelkapitän* of 4./JG 53 the following month. He would reach his half-century with a Spitfire downed over Normandy on 2 July

But the *Gruppe*'s own losses were becoming prohibitive. And on 12 July, having suffered 20 pilots killed or missing, plus another 16 wounded – the equivalent of almost an entire *Gruppe* establishment – the survivors were withdrawn to Hustedt, north of Hannover, for rest and re-equipment. 'Rest and re-equipment' was, however, no longer the restorative process that it had been in the earlier war years. Now it was simply a question of making up numbers.

True, II./JG 53 did receive a batch of brand new Bf 109G-14 fighters, but the replacement pilots drafted in to fly them were almost all young and hopelessly inexperienced. In an effort to ease the situation, one or two veteran NCOs were added to their ranks. Among them was Oberfeldwebel Alexander Preinfalk, a 74-victory Knight's Cross-wearing *Experte* from JG 77 who had latterly been serving as a fighter instructor.

Its strength increased in the interim to four *Staffeln*, Hauptmann Meimberg's II./JG 53 was returned to France in the third week of August. It immediately became apparent that numbers alone were not enough. On 22 August the *Gruppe* suffered its worst day of the entire Normandy campaign when it lost seven G-14s in a fierce dogfight with P-38s over its own base at La Fere, south of St Quentin. Five dead and two wounded was a high price to pay in exchange for the nine US fighters claimed during the course of the day's three missions.

The Battle of Normandy was already lost, not only in the air but also on the ground. On 28 August American tanks were reported to be approaching La Fere. Twenty-four hours later, just ten days after arriving back in France, II./JG 53's surviving *Gustavs* took off under fire from the leading enemy tanks. And this time they were leaving for good, heading first for Chievres, in Belgium, and then on to Eindhoven, in the Netherlands. A heavy bombing raid on 3 September that rendered Eindhoven almost unusable finally resulted in the *Gruppe*'s transfer back to Germany.

While II./JG 53 was being driven out of France, another of JG 53's *Gruppen* was being forced to evacuate Rumania, more than 1200 miles to the east.

Hauptmann Jürgen Harder's I./JG 53 had been transferred from Italy to Rumania at the beginning of May 1944. Based at Targsorul-Nou, it was to help strengthen the defences of the oil refineries at nearby Ploesti. And initially its operations – like those of II. *Gruppe* when first stationed in Austria – were simply a continuation of the campaign it had been waging against the Fifteenth Air Force flying in from the Mediterranean.

After a brief skirmish with a formation of B-17s in poor weather on 18 May, I./JG 53's first major confrontation with the Fifteenth Air Force in this new theatre occurred on the last day of the month. It ended in claims for seven B-24s and a single P-51 without any losses in return. Further successes were recorded in June. On the 6th – D-Day in the west – it was credited with another seven Liberators near Ploesti, but this time lost a pilot of 1. *Staffel* to the bombers' escorting Mustangs.

On 10 June I./JG 53 intercepted a dive-bombing raid on one of the Ploesti refineries by Italy-based P-38s. This little known operation, believed to be the longest such undertaken in the Mediterranean, proved costly for the two Lightning groups involved. They lost a total of 22 of their aircraft, at least six of which fell victim to pilots of I./JG 53.

Indicative of I./JG 53's changing fortunes – and opponents – during its time in Rumania, *Gruppenkommandeur* Jürgen Harder's successes were neatly divided between, first, eight American machines (six P-51s and a brace of B-24s) and then five Soviet (four Yak-9s and a single Il-2 *Sturmovik*)

The *Gruppe*'s most successful day in Rumania took place on 28 June when it claimed eight B-24s and a pair of P-51s close to the country's capital, Bucharest. But these victories were offset by the loss of two of its own pilots missing and four wounded. 28 June 1944 would also prove to be the last occasion in the unit's history when a daily total reached double figures.

In an attempt to improve the Luftwaffe's defensive performance, several units currently protecting Rumania's vital oil industry (including II./JG 51, III./JG 77 and elements of JG 301) had been combined with the now Major Jürgen Harder's I./JG 53 to form the *Gefechtsverband* 'Harder' (Combat Command Harder). But such measures counted for little against the growing strength of the Fifteenth Air Force. Luftwaffe losses rose sharply in July, culminating on the last day of the month, which, in Major Harder's own words, had been 'A critical day – 23 of my 32 machines were shot down. It was terrible. We were opposed by about 150 enemy fighters'.

These figures obviously refer to the entire *Gefechtsverband* (all 32 of them!), for I./JG 53's losses in the savage dogfight with the P-51s over the Rumanian-Bulgarian border region on that 31 July had been four killed or missing, and two wounded.

But, as with II./JG 53 in Normandy, it was events on the ground, not losses in the air, that were to determine the *Gruppe*'s immediate future – although, in Rumania, these events were concerned not so much with the actual fighting, as with the host country's abrupt change of sides. The Red Army had reached the pre-war frontier between the USSR and Rumania back at the beginning of April. But it was a new Soviet offensive, launched on 22 August, that finally tipped the balance. Hostilities between Rumania and the Allies ceased 48 hours later, and on 25 August the Rumanians declared war on Germany.

I./JG 53 exchanged one lot of opponents for another almost overnight. After claiming a P-51 escorting a raid on Ploesti on 18 August, Major Harder led his *Gruppe* to northern Rumania to begin operations against the Red Air Force. During the course of a *freie Jagd* mission on 20 August, he was credited with a pair of Yak-9s and a single Il-2 *Sturmovik* (victories 59-61 on his score sheet). But Rumania's sudden transfer of allegiance made I./JG 53's position in the country untenable. Having returned to Targsorul-Nou, near Ploesti, on 25 August, the *Gruppe* took off from there the following afternoon – under artillery fire from their erstwhile comrades in arms – and set course for Budak, in southern Hungary.

Some two months prior to this, towards the end of June 1944, the last two components of JG 53 – Major Bennemann's *Geschwaderstab* and Major Götz's III. *Gruppe* – had finally been withdrawn from Italy. While the former was sent on a brief, but ultimately ineffective, deployment to the eastern front (to try to help organise the aerial defence of northern Poland in the face of the Red Army's massive 1944 summer offensive), III./JG 53 returned to Germany. Initially based at Bad Lippspringe, near Paderborn, it was to spend the next few weeks training new – and inevitably mostly green – young pilots for their forthcoming role in Defence of the Reich operations.

Unlike II. and I./JG 53's early operations in Austria and Rumania, however, III. *Gruppe* did not enjoy the benefit of a 'running-in' period

'Black 11' of 8./JG 53 warms up its engine during III. *Gruppe*'s brief period of training at Bad Lippspringe in the summer of 1944. This is believed to be the machine of Unteroffizier (later Oberfeldwebel) Heinz Girnth, who had already claimed two kills over Italy, and would add a further nine during Defence of the Reich operations

against the familiar foes of the Fifteenth Air Force, but was sent up against the 'Mighty Eighth' immediately upon completion of its training. And the pilots' soaring casualty returns fully reflected this fact – 29 July, one pilot wounded, 3 August, two killed and one wounded, 4 August, nine killed or missing and two wounded. Among the five killed on the latter date was the 50-victory Oberleutnant Franz Barten, *Kapitän* of 9. *Staffel*, who was shot in his parachute after combat with a group of P-47s near Soltau. Barten's Knight's Cross, awarded on 24 October, and his promotion to hauptmann would both be posthumous.

Although III./JG 53 had claimed four B-17s and twice that number of their escorting fighters during the actions of 3 and 4 August, it was the steady drain of the *Gruppe*'s own losses that was to mark the next six weeks. On 6 August it moved to Sachau, where, in line with other Defence of the Reich *Jagdgruppen*, it was to be brought up to four-*Staffel* strength (in the event, the new 12./JG 53 would not be activated until early September at Mörtitz).

22 August was to prove an exceptionally full day. In the morning the *Gruppe* was first despatched with all urgency to Stubendorf, near Vienna, Luftwaffe intelligence having presumably got wind of an impending raid on the area by the Fifteenth Air Force. Following a fairly inconclusive two hours in the air – and a single P-51 claimed by *Kommandeur* Franz Götz (his 53rd) – its pilots then landed around midday at Brünn (Brno), in Czechoslovakia, some 65 miles north of the Austrian capital. Several hours later, the unit was ordered to stage back northwards again, via Mörtitz, all the way to Leeuwarden, on the Dutch North Sea coast!

For now, in addition to its Reich's defence duties, III./JG 53 was also being tasked with providing *Staffeln*, on a rotational basis, to protect the coastal convoys that were still plying between the Netherlands and the ports of northern Germany.

These ancillary duties appear to have resulted in little, if any, action. It was against the ever-increasing numbers of US 'heavies' – and against all the odds – that the *Gruppe* achieved its final successes in the late summer of 1944.

On 24 August, in a 35-minute running battle high above Lüneburg Heath, Major Götz and his pilots were credited with a total of eight B-17s destroyed against one killed and three wounded. Five days later they claimed another half-dozen Flying Fortresses – this time of the Fifteenth Air Force – east of Vienna. And while these last had been brought down without loss, the *Gruppe*'s next clash with the Eighth Air Force, which resulted in the destruction of a trio of B-24s and a solitary P-47 over central southern Germany on 11 September, cost it three more killed and two wounded.

Since the death of Franz Barten over a month earlier, III./JG 53's sole high scorer had been *Kommandeur* Franz Götz, whose total was now standing at 54. But the arrival of the Oak Leaves-wearing Hauptmann Alfred Grislawski from JG 1 to take over as *Kapitän* of 11. *Staffel* meant that the 'Ace of Spades' at last had another centurion among its ranks – the first since the *Geschwader*'s days in Sicily. And it was Grislawski who was responsible for two of the four 'heavies' downed by III./JG 53 near Berlin on 12 September.

But a single outstanding *Experte*, even one with 132 victories now under his belt, could not reverse the *Gruppe*'s fortunes. The bulk of Major Götz's pilots were by this time callow youngsters with little more than three to five hours' flying time in the Bf 109. Dedicated and courageous they may have been, but they simply did not stand a chance against the highly trained combat veterans of the Eighth Air Force.

On 13 September III./JG 53 flew its final Defence of the Reich mission, claiming no successes and losing one pilot over the Kassel area. It now embarked upon the closing chapter of its story, which would see it reunited with II. *Gruppe* and operating in a tactical role defending southwest Germany against the advancing US 7th and French 1st Armies.

After making good the losses suffered in Normandy, 'Jule' Meimberg's II./JG 53 had been stationed for a short while in southern Holland. But early in September it was transferred back to Germany, firstly to Darmstadt-Griesheim and then to Lorsch, north of Mannheim. This was the very area where the *Geschwader* had spent its formative years, and over which it had flown throughout much of the 'Phoney War'. But there was nothing phoney about this sector of the Rhine by the autumn of 1944.

On its first operation from Lorsch – a sweep over eastern France on 12 September – the *Gruppe* ran into a mixed force of P-47s and P-51s near Metz and was lucky to escape with only one pilot lost. Then, five days later, an unexpected danger suddenly threatened to the north when Allied airborne troops attempted to seize the bridge over the Lower Rhine at Arnhem.

Both II. and III./JG 53 would be employed against the airborne corridor stretching across Holland's three major natural waterways from Eindhoven to Arnhem. But whereas II. *Gruppe* remained south of Frankfurt, and continued to patrol the Metz-Nancy regions of France in between flying missions up to Arnhem, Franz Götz's III./JG 53 – after moving from Mörtitz to Paderborn, little more than 100 miles from the scene of the Arnhem fighting – became part of the four *Gruppe*-strong *Gefechtsverband* 'Michalski'. The latter unit, which was one of the three combat commands set up specifically to oppose the Allied air landings, was led by Major Gerhard Michalski, long-time *Kommandeur* of II./JG 53 and now *Kommodore* of JG 4.

Brought in from JG 1 to take over as *Staffelkapitän* of 11./JG 53 and inject some much needed experience into the reorganised III./JG 53, the 130-victory *Experte* Hauptmann Alfred Grislawski was able to add just three more victories to his personal tally before being wounded in a dogfight with P-51s near Münster on 26 September 1944

Neither *Gruppe* appears to have made much impact, however. One of the few known losses was a 9. *Staffel* pilot brought down by anti-aircraft fire during a low-level attack in the Nijmegen area on 24 September. Coincidentally, this date also saw II. *Gruppe*'s first recorded success since its withdrawal from Normandy. But the RAF Dakota that Hauptmann Meimberg shot down near Ludwigshafen was not making a supply run to Arnhem – it was a ferry transport that had strayed disastrously off course during the first leg of a planned flight to India!

On 26 September III./JG 53 took off from Paderborn for another low-level sweep of the Arnhem area, only to run into a formation of P-38s before reaching the Dutch border. Although able to claim three of the Lightnings, it lost three of its own pilots killed and four wounded in the short, but intense, dogfight that immediately erupted. Among the wounded was Hauptmann Alfred Grislawski, who, after accounting for one of the P-38s – his 133rd, and last, victory of the war – was forced to bail out of his 'Black 6' near Münster. Two days later II. *Gruppe* redressed the balance somewhat when it claimed five P-47s without loss during one of its regular *freie Jagd* sweeps of the Metz-Nancy areas of southeast France.

With the failure of the Arnhem venture (the last survivors of the 1st British Airborne Division had retired back across the Lower Rhine on 27 September), II and III./JG 53 were finally reunited under Oberstleutnant Bennemann's *Geschwaderstab*, which had long returned from its abortive foray to the eastern front. For the remaining months of the war their activities would be concentrated almost entirely on supporting the German ground forces defending the southwestern area of Germany.

Their operations would consist in the main of low-level attacks on enemy troops and armour, scouring the wooded hills and valleys of the Vosges and Black Forest regions either side of the Rhine for the Allies' small, but potentially lethal, artillery spotting aircraft and – above all – trying to protect their own troops from the attentions of the ever-present P-47 and P-51 fighter-bombers patrolling the skies overhead. And to assist them in these tasks an extra *Gruppe* was added to Bennemann's command in the third week of October.

IV./JG 53 was brought into being by redesignating III./JG 76, which itself had been created out of a defunct *Zerstörergruppe* only three months earlier. In the interim the unit had suffered heavy losses on the western front and was now made up almost wholly of inexperienced and poorly trained personnel. Its addition to the ranks of JG 53 therefore served little more purpose than to provide extra cannon fodder for marauding US fighters. Over the next ten weeks, together with the inevitable casualties among the younger rank and file, two of its *Gruppenkommandeure* and four *Staffelkapitäne* would be killed in action.

On 29 October, five days after Hauptmann Julius Meimberg had been awarded the Knight's Cross (for his then total of 45), all three *Gruppen* took to the air together for the first time. They had been ordered to fly a *freie Jagd* sweep along the Rhine front between Mannheim and Karlsruhe. But, as was invariably the case by this stage, they ran foul of large numbers of enemy fighters along the way.

After a series of long and scrappy engagements east of the Rhine, they submitted claims for no fewer than seven P-51s and a single P-47 (one of

Late in October the long-serving Hauptmann Julius Meimberg, whose 11./JG 2 had been incorporated into the *Geschwader* at the start of the Tunisian campaign, and who was now *Kommandeur* of II./JG 53, was presented with the Knight's Cross by Oberst Karl Hentschel, Officer Commanding 5. *Jagddivision* (left), while staff officer Oberstleutnant Siegfried von Eschwege looked on. Although reportedly awarded for 40 victories, Meimberg's score by this stage was rapidly approaching the half-century. On Meimberg's face is scarring caused by the severe burns he sustained over Tunisia in early 1943

the former providing Oberstleutnant Helmut Bennemann with his 92nd, and final, victory of the war). But it had cost them ten of their own killed and four wounded. Perhaps not surprisingly, IV./JG 53 were hit particularly hard, losing both *Gruppenkommandeur* Hauptmann Hans Morr and the *Kapitän* of his 13. *Staffel* to Mustangs in the Karlsruhe area.

Weather permitting, JG 53 continued to fly *freie Jagd* and anti-fighter bomber sorties along the Strasbourg-Colmar sectors west of the Rhine in November. But successes were few – just three in all, including a Piper Cub on the 25th for 6. *Staffel*'s Leutnant Herbert Rollwage (his 70th). In the same period the *Geschwader* sustained more than 20 casualties to all causes, including three killed and five wounded on 18 November alone.

December 1944 was, of course, to be dominated by Hitler's surprise counter-offensive through the Ardennes. Based well to the south of the 'Bulge', JG 53's three *Gruppen* were not directly involved in the Ardennes fighting. But they were perhaps even worse off than those units that were. As the only Luftwaffe fighter presence along the Rhine front from the area of Mainz right down to the Swiss border, it was estimated that by the end of the year they were facing odds in the air of some 100-to-1!

One of December's 37 losses was Oberfeldwebel 'Alex' Preinfalk, the *Experte* brought in from JG 77 to inject a little more experience and muscle into II. *Gruppe*. In a low-level, head-to-head duel with a P-47 northwest of Karlsruhe on 12 December, Preinfalk's fire took out his opponent – his 80th victory – but his own G-14 was also damaged. Although he bailed out, there was insufficient altitude for his parachute to open properly.

Yet despite everything, successes were still being achieved, even at this late stage. On 24 December Bennemann's pilots were credited with bringing down five B-26s. And the third of a trio of P-47s claimed by the now Major Meimberg 48 hours later took the *Kommandeur* of II. *Gruppe* to his half-century. Unfortunately, debris from this last victim hit Meimberg's own machine and he was wounded by another Thunderbolt while in the process of bailing out. After landing in open country to the west of Stuttgart, 'Jule' Meimberg was taken to a nearby farmhouse and a local doctor sent for. Arriving by bicycle, this worthy turned out to be the physician father of Hauptmann Erich 'Bubi' Hartmann, the Luftwaffe's top-ranking fighter pilot!

Meimberg's three Thunderbolts were among the last of the some 80 victories – the overwhelming majority of them P-47s and P-51s – that had been claimed by JG 53 since commencing operations in the southwest of the Reich in September. This impressive total had, however, cost the *Jagdgeschwader* nearly 100 of its own number. And the most costly operation of all was yet to come.

Operation *Bodenplatte* ('Baseplate'), the ill-considered 1945 New Year's Day attack by the Luftwaffe's fighter arm on Allied airfields in continental Europe, brought about the end of the unified aerial defence of the Reich. Ten *Jagdgeschwader* were each allotted a specific target. All but one of these were located in the Low Countries. The sole exception was that assigned to JG 53. Because of their geographical separation from the main body of Reich's Defence units based further to the north, Oberstleutnant Bennemann's three *Gruppen* were to attack the Metz area in eastern France – the scene of many of their recent operations – whose airfields now housed American P-47s.

Eager to strike back at the enemy *Jabos* that had been making their life such misery of late, the *Geschwader* was determined to put as many aircraft as possible into the air on the morning of 1 January 1945. The first to take-off, from Kirrlach, on the eastern bank of the Rhine at about 0830 hrs, were some two-dozen G-14s of III. *Gruppe*. The pilots flying these aircraft had the most distant target to attack – the field at Etain, approximately 28 miles northwest of Metz.

But, true to form, they ran into a crowd of Thunderbolts before even leaving German airspace and were prevented from reaching their objective. Instead, they found themselves involved in an untidy dogfight over Pirmasens. And although able to claim two of the P-47s, eight of their own *Gustavs* were shot down and two others forced to belly-land (the enthusiastic Americans submitted claims for 15 destroyed and 10 damaged). Fortunately, casualties were confined to just two wounded.

Taken sometime in January 1945, this well-known photograph of the remains of 13. *Staffel*'s 'White 13', a casualty of Operation *Bodenplatte*, offers no clue as to the fate of its pilot, who was officially declared missing . . .

. . . but this – perhaps fortunately rather blurred – snapshot tells the story. American GIs, including an MP, surround the belly-landed G-14/AS. The body of Unteroffizier Herbert Maxis lies sprawled on the ground, shot as he climbed out of the cockpit. Someone has already 'liberated' his flying boots

Some 15 minutes behind III./JG 53, II. and IV. *Gruppen* took off from Malmsheim and Stuttgart-Echterdingen respectively. Led by the *Geschwaderstab* under Helmut Bennemann, the 54-strong force headed for the main Metz-Frescaty airfield, which they reached virtually intact and where they inflicted substantial material damage (including the total destruction of 22 P-47s). But although they had avoided contact with Allied fighters during their approach flight, they suffered heavily at the hands of Metz-Frescaty's anti-aircraft defences.

Among the three wounded was the *Kommodore*, who nevertheless managed to land safely back at Echterdingen. Five others were captured after coming down on Allied territory – four of them over the target area, one of whom died of his injuries the following day. And a further nine were either killed or posted missing. In exchange for these 17 casualties, each *Gruppe* claimed just one aerial victory. Leutnant Karl Broo, the *Staffelkapitän*

Another victim of US anti-aircraft fire during the New Year's Day attack on Metz-Frescaty airfield, engine damage forced Gefreiter Alfred Michel of 16./JG 53 down southwest of Merzig, some 16 kilometres from the spot where the hapless Maxis landed. If not altogether cordial, Michel's reception certainly was not lethal. He has even had his head injury, sustained when he was thrown forward against the *Revi* gun sight, bandaged – as may be seen from this photograph of him ruefully surveying the wreckage of the 'Blue 2' in which he had just flown his first and last operational mission

179-victory *Experte* Hauptmann Helmut Lipfert, hitherto the *Staffelkapitän* of 6./JG 52, was not exactly overjoyed at being appointed *Kommandeur* of I./JG 53, part of a unit that he had publicly stated had 'long outlived its former glory'

of 8./JG 53, who was leading the II. *Gruppe* formation in place of the wounded 'Jule' Meimberg, was credited with a Spitfire – possibly French-flown. And Oberfeldwebel Eduard Isken of 13. *Staffel* (another ex-JG 77 alumnus, and one of IV./JG 53's very few experienced pilots) downed an unwary Auster AOP aircraft that he encountered *en route* to Metz, and which presented him with his 50th.

After the *Bodenplatte* debacle, in which many of the northern *Jagdgeschwader* had achieved much less and suffered far greater losses than JG 53, most of the Defence of the Reich units were sent to the eastern front in a desperate attempt to halt the advancing tide of the Red Army. But JG 53 was kept firmly in place in southwest Germany, denying Oberstleutnant Bennemann any last chance of gathering his itinerant I. *Gruppe* back into the *Geschwader* fold.

Since being forced to evacuate Rumania back in September, Major Jürgen Harder's I./JG 53 had been conducting a fighting withdrawal through Hungary. Its operations were a mirror image of those being flown by Bennemann's western-based *Gruppen* – *freie Jagd* and ground-attack escort missions, while at the same time trying to protect its own ground forces against the enemy's absolute air superiority. The only differences were the terrain – the flat plains of Hungary in place of the rolling hills of the Rhineland – and its opponents, which were heavily armoured *Sturmovik* ground-assault aircraft instead of ubiquitous P-47s and P-51s.

But I./JG 53 also differed from the other *Gruppen* in its rate of scoring. Before final disbandment, it would be credited with almost 130 enemy aircraft destroyed. Its own casualties would number less than two dozen from all causes, including just five reported killed or missing in action. As always, however, individual successes in the air had little influence on events unfolding on the ground. The Red Army was unstoppable, and its next objective was Budapest. The offensive began on 8 December, and by the 26th the Hungarian capital was surrounded.

The city was under siege for the next seven weeks, before finally falling to the Soviets on 11 February 1945. It became the focal point for many of the *Gruppe*'s operations during this time. Its fighters not only patrolled above those areas of the capital held by German forces, but also escorted Ju 87 dive-bombers trying to break the Red Army's stranglehold on the city and – when this failed – flew cover for the transport Heinkels dropping supplies to the beleaguered defenders.

Towards the end of January 1945, Major Jürgen Harder was appointed *Kommodore* of JG 11. He was the last of the *Gruppe*'s original high scorers (his 65th kill, an La-5, had gone down on 4 January). But the victories already amassed by the second of two acting-*Kommandeure* drafted in temporarily to replace him eclipsed this total more than fivefold, for he was none other than Hauptmann Erich Hartmann, the Luftwaffe's highest scoring *Experte*. Unfortunately, he did not remain long at the head of I./JG 53. After ordering all the *Gruppe*'s *Gustavs* to be painted a drab grey-white (the better to blend in with the wintry landscape below) and pausing only to shoot down a Yak-9 on 4 February (his 337th!), 'Bubi' Hartmann quickly departed whence he came – back to JG 52.

Jürgen Harder's official successor, Hauptmann Helmut Lipfert, arrived on 15 February. Like Hartmann, the 179-victory Lipfert had previously served solely with JG 52. Harder's I./JG 53 had been operating alongside elements of JG 52 in recent months, but, not surprisingly, the newcomers' performance had failed to match up to that of the eastern front veterans. Helmut Lipfert certainly did not think so, and was none too happy about his new appointment;

'I am supposed to take over from Hartmann as *Kommandeur* of I./JG 53, a *Gruppe* from a *Geschwader* that has long outlived its former glory.'

Lipfert would later go so far as to suggest that I./JG 53 should be disbanded and he be sent back to JG 52 as a *Staffelkapitän*. But, like it or not, he was to remain in office for the last two months of the *Gruppe*'s existence – and even succeeded in taking his final score to 203 while so doing.

With the capture of Budapest, the Soviets' next objective was clearly Vienna. Early March thus found I./JG 53 based at Veszprem, near Hungary's Lake Balaton, guarding the southeastern approaches to the Austrian capital. But nothing could now halt the Red Army's juggernaut advance, and by month-end the *Gruppe* had been driven back to the Hungarian-Austrian border. On 2 April I./JG 53's strength was divided, part withdrawing to Vienna-Seyring, part to Fels am Wagram, some 30 miles further to the west.

It was over the Vienna area that the *Gruppe*'s final missions would be flown. On 8 April Hauptmann Lipfert claimed the Lavochkin fighter that took him to his double century. But another feat on that selfsame day – if true – was even more remarkable. It would seem that a leutnant of 2. *Staffel*, not scheduled to fly, had partaken a little too freely of what the celebrated wine cellars of Fels had to offer, only then to be informed that he was down for a *freie Jagd* sweep.

Over the outskirts of Vienna the *Gustavs* ran into a large gaggle of Soviet fighters and, according to eye-witnesses, the leutnant 'hurled himself at the Russians like a madman, firing with everything he had'. After a shaky

These two photographs of late model, Erla-hooded *Gustavs* of I./JG 53 abandoned. . .

**. . . and surrendered in April 1945 show that I. *Gruppe*'s machines in the east bore the 'Ace of Spades' badge right up until the end . . .**

landing back at Fels, his machine rolled to a halt in the middle of the field, and he was seen to slump forward in his seat. Fearing the worst, the other members of the *Gruppe* rushed to his aid – only to find him sound asleep. When woken, he could not even remember flying the mission, let alone shooting down a trio of Yak-3s!

Two days later I./JG 53 lost its last aircraft when Oberleutnant Hans Kornatz, the *Kapitän* of 1. *Staffel*, came off second best in a fight with an Il-2 over Vienna and had to put his 'White 5' down in a spectacular belly landing amid the rubble of one of the city's main thoroughfares. Kornatz, whose 36th and final victory had been a Rumanian Bf 109 downed on 25 February, was the last remaining member of I./JG 53 to have been with the *Gruppe* since its formation in 1937. His writing-off the G-10 in the ruins of Vienna was almost symbolic, for just six days later, on 16 April, Hauptmann Lipfert claimed I./JG 53's last victory – a Yak-9. Twenty-four hours after that, he got both his Oak Leaves and, presumably, his dearest wish – the *Gruppe* was disbanded.

While I./JG 53 had been retreating through Hungary into Austria, Helmut Bennemann's three other *Gruppen* had likewise been giving ground as they were pushed back across southern Germany. And theirs was to prove much the costlier of the two withdrawals. On the day after *Bodenplatte*, they lost another five pilots to Allied fighters, including Hauptmann Friedrich Müer, the *Kommandeur* of IV./JG 53, shot down by P-51s as he came in to land at Stuttgart. In the next four months prior to their final surrender, they would suffer a further 47 killed or missing. And these, together with the 40 captured or wounded, meant that their overall casualty figures came very close to equalling the number of enemy aircraft – still predominantly P-47s and P-51s – that they claimed during the same period.

Although JG 53 had played no direct part in the Ardennes campaign, it was called upon to support Operation *Nordwind* – the subsequent, but far less ambitious, German counter-offensive in northern Alsace that had been launched on 31 December 1944. But, like the 'Bulge', *Nordwind* also quickly ground to a halt in the face of stiffening Allied opposition.

. . . whereas the western-based *Gruppen* had removed the famous symbol from their fighters late in 1944, as witness this G-14 of 12. *Staffel* running up its engine at a wintry, wooded Kirrlach in mid-January 1945

However, weather permitting – and January 1945 was to be a month of heavy snow and very poor conditions – the *Geschwader* continued to support German troops holding out on the west bank of the Rhine.

During this period JG 53 was honoured with its last Knight's Cross when Eduard Isken, the veteran oberfeldwebel brought in from JG 77 to add his experience to IV. *Gruppe*, received the award on 14 January with a score still standing at 50 (the half-century having been provided by the hapless Auster shot out of the sky during *Bodenplatte*). Three days after this, another long-serving *Gruppenkommandeur* was lost to the *Geschwader* when III./JG 53's Major Franz Götz departed to take command of JG 26. His place at the head of III. *Gruppe* was filled by Hauptmann Siegfried Luckenbach, hitherto *Kapitän* of 12. *Staffel*.

When the weather finally began to improve in the middle of February 1945, it brought with it an immediate escalation in losses among both pilots and aircraft. On 22 February Bennemann's *Gruppen* suffered five killed or missing, four wounded and 17 Bf 109G/Ks lost or damaged. Twenty-four hours later, exactly the same number of casualties were incurred – again mainly in combat with US fighters – while the total number of machines lost or damaged rose to 20.

Attrition on this scale could not be borne for long. Early in March each *Gruppe* was reduced back down to three-*Staffel* strength with the disbandment of 8., 12. and 16./JG 53. By now they were operating over their own cities to the east of the Rhine. The war was irretrievably lost, but the Luftwaffe leadership refused to accept the fact. On 8 March Hermann Göring dispatched a top-secret telex calling for volunteers for the near suicidal *Rammkommando* Elbe operation (see *Osprey Aviation Elite Units 20 - Luftwaffe Sturmgruppen* for further details). Hauptmann Luckenbach's III./JG 53 reportedly volunteered *en masse*, although in the event their apparent fervour was never put to the test. 'Jule' Meimberg's cooler head dissuaded the pilots of his II. *Gruppe* from following suit.

Instead, JG 53 was transferred closer to the middle Rhine sector, where US troops had unexpectedly seized a bridge across the river at Remagen. But after several days of costly missions in this area, the *Gruppen* returned to the Stuttgart region. So absolute was Allied air superiority by this stage that Bennemann's pilots could now only operate during the hours of dawn and dusk. And still they were being forced to retreat.

Oberstleutnant Helmut Bennemann's last Order of the Day to the *Geschwader* – dated 24 April 1945 – in which he paid tribute to the 600 pilots and 241 members of the ground staff who had lost their lives during the war, closed with the words 'A *'Horridoh'* and farewell to you all'. . .

. . . and all that remained of their passing was the wreckage of their machines – such as Bf 109K-4 'White 16' of 9./JG 53 – many of which were simply left to rot in the forests of southern Germany for years after the final surrender

On 27 March II./JG 53 began the move to Ulm-Risstissen. The following week III. and IV. *Gruppen* retired further eastward still into Bavaria. But nowhere were they safe from Allied bombing and strafing. On 17 April – the day I./JG 53 was disbanded in Austria – all three western *Gruppen* flew a series of *freie Jagd* and ground-attack sorties across a broad swathe of Upper Bavaria, but with little tangible result.

Three days later II./JG 53's airfield at Ulm suffered a devastating raid by B-26 bombers that left the *Gruppe* with just three serviceable G-14s. Unlike III. and IV./JG 53, who had been slowly replacing their G-14s with new Bf 109K-4s since the turn of the year, Major Meimberg's *Gruppe* appears to have been operating solely with late model *Gustavs*. Now, to add insult to injury, II./JG 53 was instructed to make good its Ulm losses by taking over a batch of war-weary cast-off G-4/6 trainers.

It did not have to suffer this indignity for long. Exactly a week later at Waal, approximately midway been Memmingen and Munich, II./JG 53 became the first of the western-based *Gruppen* to disband. Twelve miles away at Erbenschwang, Oberstleutnent Helmut Bennemann stood the *Geschwaderstab* down on that same 27 April. And IV./JG 53 – after having mounted an abortive attack on the bridge over the Danube at Dillingen with a handful of K-4s armed with special light-sensitive torpedo-bombs designed to detonate when they entered the bridge's shadow – ended its days at Holzkirchen near Munich on 29 April.

All of which left just III. *Gruppe* to carry out JG 53's final operations of the war along the Danube between Regensburg and Passau. The last mission of all, against columns of US trucks and armour southwest of Munich, was flown on 2 May 1945. After returning to Prien (their field just north of the Munich-Salzburg Autobahn), the remaining fighters of JG 53 were then unceremoniously doused with what little fuel was left and blown up.

The 'Ace of Spades', which had left its mark over London, Paris, Stalingrad, Rome, Budapest and Vienna, was no more. But it would not be forgotten.

# APPENDICES

## APPENDIX 1

## COMMANDING OFFICERS

### *Kommodoren*

| | | |
|---|---|---|
| Lörzer, *Oberst* Bruno | 15/3/37 | to 31/3/38 |
| Junck, *Obstlt* Werner | 1/4/38 | to 30/9/39 |
| Klein, *GenMaj* Hans | 1/10/39 | to 31/12/39 |
| von Cramon-Taubadel, | | |
| *Obstlt* Hans-Jürgen | 1/1/40 | to 30/9/40 |
| von Maltzahn, *Oberst* Günther | 9/10/40 | to 4/10/43 |
| Müller, *Maj* Friedrich-Karl (acting) | 10/43 | to 10/43 |
| Ubben, *Maj* Kurt (acting) | 10/43 | to 11/43 |
| Bennemann, *Obstlt* Helmut | 9/11/43 | to 27/4/45 |

### *Gruppenkommandeure*

#### I./JG 53

| | | |
|---|---|---|
| von Blomberg, *Hptm* Alexander | 1/10/37 | to 31/10/38 |
| Witt, *Maj* Hans-Hugo | 1/11/38 | to 30/4/39 |
| von Janson, *Hptm* Lothar | 1/5/39 | to 30/6/40 |
| Blumensaat, *Hptm* Albert | 1/7/40 | to 25/8/40 |
| Mayer, *Hptm* Hans-Karl | 1/9/40 | to 17/10/40 (†) |
| Prestele, *Olt* Ignaz (acting) | 10/40 | to 10/40 |
| Brustelling, *Hptm* Hans-Heinrich | 10/40 | to 31/5/41 |
| Balfanz, *Olt* Wilfried | 1/6/41 | to 24/6/41 (†) |
| von Werra, *Hptm* Franz | 7/41 | to 25/10/41 (†) |
| Prestele, *Hptm* Ignaz (acting) | 8/41 | to 9/41 |
| Kaminski, *Maj* Herbert | 1/11/41 | to 24/7/42 (W) |
| Spies, *Hptm* Walter | 8/42 | to 10/42 |
| Müller, *Maj* Friedrich-Karl | 11/42 | to 14/2/44 |
| Harder, *Maj* Jürgen | 15/2/44 | to 1/45 |
| Ernst, *Hptm* Wolfgang (acting) | 1/45 | to 2/45 |
| Hartmann, *Hptm* Erich (acting) | 2/45 | to 15/2/45 |
| Lipfert, *Hptm* Helmut | 15/2/45 | to 17/4/45 |

#### II./JG 53

| | | |
|---|---|---|
| von Rohden, | | |
| *Maj* Hans-Detlev Herhudt | 15/3/37 | to 30/6/37 |
| von Bernegg, *Maj* Hubert Merhart | 1/7/37 | to 18/8/39 |
| von Maltzahn, *Hptm* Günther | 19/8/39 | to 8/10/40 |
| Bretnütz, *Hptm* Heinz | 9/10/40 | to 27/6/41 (†) |
| Spies, *Hptm* Walter | 6/41 | to 7/42 |
| Michalski, *Maj* Gerhard | 7/42 | to 23/4/44 |
| Westphal, *Hptm* Hans-Jürgen (acting) | 19/6/43 | to 7/43 |
| Schnell, *Maj* Karl-Heinz (acting) | 7/43 | to 28/9/43 |
| Meimberg, *Maj* Julius | 24/4/44 | to 27/4/45 |

#### III./JG 53

| | | |
|---|---|---|
| Mölders, *Hptm* Werner | 3/10/39 | to 5/6/40 (PoW) |
| Pingel, *Hptm* Rolf (acting) | 6/40 | to 20/6/40 |
| Harder, *Hptm* Harro | 7/40 | to 12/8/40 (†) |
| Wilcke, *Maj* Wolf-Dietrich | 13/8/40 | to 18/5/42 |
| Gerlitz, *Hptm* Erich | 5/42 | to 10/42 |
| Götz, *Maj* Franz | 10/42 | to 17/1/45 |
| Luckenbach, *Hptm* Siegfried | 18/1/45 | to 2/5/45 |
| Ernst, *Hptm* Wolfgang (acting) | 4/45 | to 2/5/45 |

#### IV./JG 53

| | | |
|---|---|---|
| Morr, *Hptm* Hans | 25/10/44 | to 29/10/44 (†) |
| Müer, *Hptm* Friedrich | 30/10/44 | to 2/1/45 (†) |
| Hammer, *Hptm* Alfred | 9/1/45 | to 29/4/45 |

(†) – Killed or Missing

(PoW) – Prisoner of War

(W) Wounded

# APPENDIX 2

## AWARD WINNERS

| Date | Name | Unit | Award | Score at Time of Award | Total Score | Fate |
|---|---|---|---|---|---|---|
| 29/5/40 | Mölders, *Hptm* Werner | III. | KC | 20 | 101 | KAS |
| 3/9/40 | Mayer, *Hptm* Hans-Karl | I. | KC | 20 | 31 | MiA |
| 22/10/40 | Bretnütz, *Hptm* Heinz | II. | KC | 20 | 33 | DoW |
| 30/12/40 | von Maltzahn, *Maj* Günther *Freiherr* | 53 | KC | 13 | 68 | |
| 23/7/41 | Schmidt, *Lt* Erich | 9. | KC | 30 | 47 | MiA |
| 24/7/41 | von Maltzahn, *Maj* Günther *Freiherr* | 53 | OL | 42 | 68 | |
| 6/8/41 | Schramm, *Lt* Herbert | 8. | KC | 24 | 42 | KiA |
| 6/8/41 | Wilcke, *Hptm* Wolf-Dietrich | III. | KC | 25 | 162 | KiA |
| 14/9/41 | Müller, *Oblt* Friedrich-Karl | III. | KC | 22 | 140 | KAS |
| 16/6/42 | Neuhoff, *Lt* Hermann | 7. | KC | 40 | 40 | PoW |
| 13/8/42 | Stumpf, *Ofw* Werner | 9. | KC | 40 | 47 | KiA |
| 3/9/42 | Zellot, *Lt* Walter | 2. | KC | 84 | 85 | KiA |
| 4/9/42 | Götz, *Oblt* Franz | 9. | KC | 40 | 63 | |
| 4/9/42 | Michalski, *Oblt* Gerhard | II. | KC | 41 | 73 | |
| 6/9/42 | Belser, *Hptm* Helmut | 8. | KC* | 36 | 36 | KAS |
| 6/9/42 | Tonne, *Oblt* Wolfgang | 3. | KC | 73 | 122 | KAS |
| 23/9/42 | Crinius, *Fw* Wilhelm | 3. | KC | 100 | 114 | PoW |
| 23/9/42 | Crinius, *Fw* Wilhelm | 3. | OL | 100 | 114 | PoW |
| 23/9/42 | Müller, *Oblt* Friedrich-Karl | 1. | OL | 100 | 140 | KAS |
| 24/9/42 | Tonne, *Oblt* Wolfgang | 3. | OL | 101 | 122 | KAS |
| 2/10/42 | Roehrig, *Lt* Hans | 3. | KC | 51 | 71 | MiA |
| 29/10/42 | Franke, *Ofw* Alfred | 2. | KC* | 59 | 59 | KiA |
| 23/12/42 | Dinger, *Lt* Fritz | 4. | KC | 49 | 67 | KAS |
| 30/12/42 | Golinski, *Ofw* Heinz | 3. | KC* | 47 | 47 | MiA |
| 21/6/43 | Litjens, *Ofw* Stefan | 4. | KC | 31 | 38 | W |
| 21/6/43 | Schiess, *Oblt* Franz | 8. | KC | 54 | 67 | MiA |
| 5/12/43 | Harder, *Hptm* Jürgen | 7. | KC | 40 | 64 | KAS |
| 26/3/44 | Seeger, *Lt* Günther | 7. | KC | 46 | 56 | |
| 6/4/44 | Ehrenberger, *Ofw* Rudolf | 6. | KC* | 49 | 49 | KiA |
| 6/4/44 | Rollwage, *Ofw* Herbert | 5. | KC | 53 | 102 | |
| 24/10/44 | Barten, *Oblt* Franz | 9. | KC* | 52 | 52 | KiA |
| 24/10/44 | Meimberg, *Hptm* Julius | II. | KC | 45 | 59 | |
| 14/1/45 | Isken, *Ofw* Eduard | 13./1. | KC | 50 | 56 | |
| 17/4/45 | Lipfert, *Hptm* Helmut | I. | OL | 203 | 203 | |

**Key**

KiA – Killed in Action

MiA – Missing in Action

KAS – Killed on Active Service

DoW – Died of Wounds

PoW – Prisoner of War

W – Wounded

* – awarded posthumously

KC – Knight's Cross

OL – Oak Leaves

# COLOUR PLATES

## 1

**Ar 68E 'White 11' of 3./JG 334, Mecklenburg, North Germany, Autumn 1937**

Unlike most *Jagdgeschwader* of the pre-war biplane era, at least six of which are known to have used coloured trim as a form of unit identification, the Arados of JG 334 simply retained their basic grey finish overall. Ar 68E 'White 11's' 3. *Staffel* parentage is indicated by the yellow spinner tip and the white discs on the engine cowling, aft fuselage and (just visible) the dorsal spine. The red discs partially obscuring the national insignia are, however, a purely temporary measure to show that I./JG 334 was part of 'Red Force' defending northern Germany during the large scale military manoeuvres of Autumn 1937.

## 2

**Bf 109D-1 'Red 1' of Oberleutnant Rolf Pingel, *Staffelkapitän* 2./JG 334, Wiesbaden-Erbenheim, October 1938**

I./JG 334 retained its cloak of anonymity after converting to early model Bf 109s, the only concession to individuality here being the red numeral and spinner tip denoting a 2. *Staffel* machine. After achieving ten victories while at the head of 2./JG 53, the then Hauptmann Pingel was appointed *Gruppenkommandeur* of I./JG 26 in August 1940. Today, he is best remembered – perhaps a trifle unfairly – as the man who presented RAF intelligence with the first intact model of the new Bf 109F when engine damage forced him to belly-land in Kent on 10 July 1941.

## 3

**Bf 109E 'White 5' of Unteroffizier Stefan Litjens, 4./JG 53, Mannheim-Sandhofen, October 1939**

JG 53's *'Pik-As'* ('Ace of Spades') badge was introduced shortly after the outbreak of war. It is modelled here by Unteroffizier Litjens' 'White 5', which also sports the distinctive three-tone green camouflage finish (with signs of additional overpainting in the area of the fuselage cross) worn by II. *Gruppe*'s machines during the early months of hostilities. After scoring 23 victories with 4. *Staffel*, 'Steff' Litjens was severely wounded in Russia on 11 September 1941, losing the sight of his right eye. He nonetheless resumed operational flying just over a year later, and would claim a further 15 kills before another injury threatened his remaining eye and brought an end to his combat career in March 1944.

## 4

**Bf 109E 'White 1' of Oberleutnant Wolf-Dietrich Wilcke, *Staffelkapitän* 7./JG 53, Wiesbaden-Erbenheim, October 1939**

Looking superficially similar to the machine above, this 'White 1' is in fact wearing the two-tone green finish favoured by III./JG 53 for much of the 'Phoney War' period. Note too the early style (narrow-bordered) fuselage cross and the tail swastika centred on the rudder hinge line. One of the Luftwaffe's outstanding fighter commanders, *'Fürst'* Wilcke gained 38 victories and the Knight's Cross with JG 53. He would add a further 124 kills, the Oak Leaves and Swords after transferring to JG 3. He was killed in action against P-51s near Brunswick on 23 March 1944.

## 5

**Ar 68F of 10.(N)/JG 72, Mannheim-Ludwigshafen, December 1939**

Although having long exchanged its own Ar 68Es for Bf 109s, JG 53 enjoyed another brief flirtation with the Arado biplane at the very beginning of the war when 10.(N)/JG 72 (an auxiliary nightfighter *Staffel* activated under the emergency programme of July 1939) was temporarily placed under the *Geschwader*'s command – hence the unit badge depicting an owl perched on the 'Ace of Spades'. The Arados carried no other individual markings, nor did they claim any nocturnal kills in the defence of Germany before being incorporated into IV.(N)/JG 2 in February 1940.

## 6

**Bf 109E 'Black Chevron-Triangle' of Hauptmann Werner Mölders, *Gruppenkommandeur* III./JG 53, Trier-Euren, March 1940**

Also displaying III. *Gruppe*'s two-tone green finish (albeit of a less angular pattern than that applied to *'Fürst'* Wilcke's machine), and still sporting pre-war style national insignia, this is an early mount of the legendary Werner Mölders. The last of the five victory bars displayed on the tailfin represents a French Morane-Saulnier MS.406 brought down near Metz on 3 March 1940. Although it was with JG 53 that Mölders achieved his first 25 kills – thereby becoming the first fighter pilot to be awarded the Knight's Cross – it was his appointment to JG 51, the *Geschwader* that would later bear his name, which set him on the road to true greatness (see *Osprey Aviation Elite Units 22 - Jagdgeschwader 51 'Mölders'* for further details).

## 7

**Bf 109E 'Red 5' of Feldwebel Hans Kornatz, 2./JG 53, Darmstadt-Griesheim, April 1940**

Another early *Emil* with a tail scoreboard marking the start of its pilot's career. But here the similarities with Mölders' machine (above) cease. The single bar adorning 'Red 5's' tailfin denotes one of the Fairey Battles of the RAF's No 150 Sqn brought down during the action of 30 September 1939. All 35 of Kornatz's future kills would also be claimed while serving with I./JG 53 (of which he remained a member throughout the war). Like many pilots, Hans Kornatz was superstitious and, whenever possible, he always flew an aircraft bearing the individual number '5'. The last of the line was a Bf 109G 10 that he belly-landed in the ruins of Vienna in March 1945.

## 8

**Bf 109E 'Black Chevron-Triangle' of Hauptmann Harro Harder, *Gruppenkommandeur* III./JG 53, Villiaze/ Guernsey, August 1940**

The one glaring difference between this *Emil* and those illustrated above is the red band that encircles the engine cowling and effectively obscures the 'Ace of Spades' unit emblem. Its introduction was allegedly part of a long-running campaign to discomfort and discredit *Geschwaderkommodore* Oberstleutnant Hans-Jürgen von Cramon-Taubadel (see text for details). The six kill bars on the tail of Harder's machine refer to earlier victories claimed with another unit prior to his assuming command of III./JG 53. He would be credited with five more successes while leading the group – three Spitfires on 11 August and two on 12 August – before he himself went down into the Channel east of the Isle of Wight on the latter date.

## 9

**Bf 109E 'White 8' of Hauptmann Hans-Karl Mayer, *Gruppenkommandeur* I./JG 53, Etaples, September 1940**
The advent of yellow engine cowlings (and rudders) as a recognition marking among Channel front *Jagdgeschwader* in the early autumn of 1940 allowed many pilots of JG 53 simply to have the unpopular red band overpainted. This was the course chosen by Hans-Karl Mayer, the newly appointed *Kommandeur* of I. *Gruppe*, although he was careful not to let the fresh coat of yellow paint hide his meticulously kept rudder scoreboard. There would be just two more kill bars added to the 29 shown here before he too was shot down over the Channel (on 17 October 1940 in a different machine to that shown here).

## 10

**Bf 109E 'Yellow 1' of Oberleutnant Walter Rupp, *Staffelkapitän* 3./JG 53, Le Touquet, October 1940**
I. *Gruppe's Jabostaffel*, 3./JG 53, also conveniently 'lost' the red band marking when the unit repainted the cowlings of its machines yellow. This particular E-4/B is believed to be the aircraft that three-victory Walter Rupp belly-landed at Manston after clashing with Spitfires on 17 October 1940 – the same day that Hauptmann Hans-Karl Mayer (above) disappeared into the Channel in an unarmed E-7.

## 11

**Bf 109E 'Black Chevron Circle' of Oberleutnant Friedrich-Karl Müller, *Gruppen-TO* III./JG 53, Le Touquet, November 1940**
Although his machine now wears the insignia of the *Gruppen* Technical Officer, Oberleutnant Müller had scored the last of the ten victories shown here – a Spitfire off Dungeness on 6 September 1940 – as a member of 8. *Staffel*. After the departure of Hans-Jürgen von Cramon-Taubadel, JG 53's new *Kommodore*, Major Günther von Maltzahn, quickly had the 'Ace of Spades' emblem reinstated. But the controversy lingered on. As a protest against the red band, III. *Gruppe* pilots had earlier overpainted the swastikas on the tailfins of their *Emils*, and 'Tutti' Müller has not yet got round to having his put back! A leading light of JG 53, the later Major Müller would score all but 22 of his victories while with the *Geschwader*. He was killed in May 1944 when *Kommodore* of JG 3.

## 12

**Bf 109F-2 'Black Chevron-Triangle and Bars' of Major Günther *Freiherr* von Maltzahn, *Geschwaderkommodore* JG 53, St Omer-Wizernes, May 1941**
After wintering in Germany for rest and re-equipment, JG 53 returned to the Channel front in the spring of 1941 with brand-new *Friedrichs*, each machine's lightly dappled grey-green finish set off by a bright yellow cowling (with the 'Ace of Spades' now firmly in place) and rudder. The scoreboard on the *Kommodore's* aircraft poses something of a mystery. Although it shows 20 victories, 'Henri' von Maltzahn's score at the end of May 1941 was standing at just 16 – the last of which, a Spitfire claimed north of

Calais, in fact remained unconfirmed. It has been suggested that four of the bars included in the score shown here refer to observation and anti-aircraft balloons brought down during the Battles of France and Britain. All 68 of the later Oberst von Maltzahn's final wartime total would be scored with JG 53.

## 13

**Bf 109F-2 'Black Chevron-Triangle' of Hauptmann Heinz Bretnütz, *Gruppenkommandeur* II./JG 53, St Omer-Clairmarais, May 1941**
The 32 kill bars here adoring the rudder of Bretnütz's machine presumably also include one claim that was subsequently disallowed, for post-war records show that his score at the end of May was 31. He would down his 32nd and last victim – a Soviet Tupolev SB-2 bomber - on 22 June 1941, the opening day of *Barbarossa*. Of interest here are the toning-down of the yellow spinner and cowling with a light green dapple, the name *Peter* carried below the cockpit and the telescope protruding through the windscreen to the right of the standard *Revi* gunsight.

## 14

**Bf 109F-2 'Black Chevron-Triangle' of Hauptmann Wolf-Dietrich Wilcke, *Gruppenkommandeur* III./JG 53, Maldeghem, June 1941**
Unlike von Maltzahn and Bretnütz above, Hauptmann Wolf-Dietrich Wilcke did not claim any successes during JG 53's brief return to the Channel front with its new *Friedrichs* in the spring of 1941. All 13 of the kill bars depicted here refer to earlier victories scored on *Emils* between November 1939 and October 1940 (see profile 4 and caption for details of 'Fürst' Wilcke's later career).

## 15

**Bf 109F-2 'Black Chevron and Circle/Bar' of Leutnant Jürgen Harder, *Gruppenstab* III./JG 53, Suwalki, June 1941**
By the start of Operation *Barbarossa*, most of III./JG 53's machines sported a wide yellow theatre marking band around the aft fuselage. This, together with the overpainting of the previously yellow engine cowling, gives Harder's *Friedrich* a totally different look from those previously illustrated in this colour section. It has been suggested that the unusual *Stab* insignia indicates that Harder was doubling up as both adjutant and TO. Note also the single kill bar on the rudder (for an 'I-17' claimed on the opening afternoon of *Barbarossa*) and the name *Harro* beneath the cockpit in memory of his dead brother.

## 16

**Bf 109F-2 'Black Chevron-Triangle and Bars' of Major Günther *Freiherr* von Maltzahn, *Geschwaderkommodore* JG 53, Byelaya-Zirkov, July 1941**
With its narrow aft fuselage band and unusually dark overall finish, this *Friedrich* – one of several flown by *Kommodore* von Maltzahn during the early weeks of the Russian campaign – offers an even more striking contrast to that depicted by profile 12. But the rudder scoreboard discrepancies remain. The first two rows of (20) kills are clearly topped by western roundels, although his confirmed pre-*Barbarossa* total is now thought to have been 15. Such was von Maltzahn's rate of scoring during July 1941, however, that only six days separate his actual score of 37 from the 42 shown here.

## 17

**Bf 109F-4 'White 4' of Leutnant Fritz Dinger, 4./JG 53, Lyuban, October 1941**

Also displaying a wide yellow aft fuselage band, this heavily mottled 'White 4' (note the unusual style of the numeral) is the mount of Fritz Dinger. Its rudder bears witness to the first ten of his final total of 67 victories, all scored with II. *Gruppe*. After being promoted to oberleutnant, assuming command of 4. *Staffel* and being awarded the Knight's Cross (for a score of 49), Fritz Dinger would be killed in a US bombing raid in Italy on 27 July 1943.

## 18

**Bf 109F-4 'Black Double Chevron' of Hauptmann Herbert Kaminski, *Gruppenkommandeur* I./JG 53, San Pietro/ Sicily, January 1942**

When I./JG 53 transferred from the eastern front to the Mediterranean late in 1941, the theatre markings changed from yellow to white, although few machines carried such a wide aft fuselage band as that depicted here (Kaminski's groundcrew had presumably simply overpainted the previous broad expanse of yellow). An ex-*Zerstörer* pilot already wearing the Knight's Cross, Herbert Kaminski scored just two victories with JG 53 – one over Malta and the second after I. *Gruppe*'s return to Russia in spring 1942. Major Kaminski was injured in an emergency landing in September 1942 and, upon recovery, returned to the *Zerstörer* arm to lead II./ZG 76 in Defence of the Reich.

## 19

**Bf 109F-4/Z 'White 1' of Oberleutnant Werner Langemann, *Staffelkapitän* 10.(*Jabo*)/JG 53, San Pietro/Sicily, January 1942**

The *Friedrichs* of 10.(*Jabo*)/JG 53, a dedicated fighter-bomber *Staffel* activated in Sicily late in January 1942, also wore a standard temperate camouflage scheme. They were distinguished by their unit badge – a bomb dropping on the island of Malta, which was carried on the rear fuselage either aft of the white theatre band (as seen here) or superimposed upon it. Werner Langemann claimed three aerial victories with JG 53 before his *Staffel* was amalgamated with 10.(*Jabo*)/JG 27 to form *Jabogruppe Afrika*, which he then commanded. After redesignation, the unit badge was amended accordingly, with the silhouette of Malta being replaced by that of Africa.

## 20

**Bf 109F-4 'Black 1' of Hauptmann Kurt Brändle, *Staffelkapitän* 5./JG 53, Comiso/Sicily, April 1942**

Shortly after arriving in the Mediterranean II./JG 53 introduced a new segmented camouflage scheme. It is still not known with certainty, however, whether this consisted of a brown/green or grey/green finish. Given the overwater nature of the *Gruppe*'s operations against Malta at this time, the latter is arguably the more likely, and is thus depicted here. Kurt Brändle scored 35 victories with JG 53 before being appointed *Gruppenkommandeur* of II./JG 3 on the eastern front and Defence of the Reich, where he would take his total to 172 prior to being killed in action over the North Sea on 3 November 1943.

## 21

**Bf 109F-4/trop 'White 5' of Leutnant Jürgen Harder, 7./JG 53, Martuba/Libya, June 1942**

No uncertainty about this scheme. After returning to Africa in May 1942, III./JG 53 quickly adopted the in-theatre camouflage finish of desert tan uppersurfaces and light blue undersides. Harder's *Friedrich* provides a copybook example. Note the somewhat over-dimensioned fuselage cross, however, and two other more individual features – the rudder scoreboard (with the last of the 17 kill bars shown here representing a South African Tomahawk claimed off Tobruk on 14 June) and the name *Harro* now more prominently displayed below the cockpit (see profile 15). Later machines would have the name of a second brother added – Rolf, also killed in action. Jürgen, the last of the three, would crash – reportedly due to oxygen failure – near Berlin on 17 February when *Kommodore* of JG 11.

## 22

**Bf 109F-4/trop 'Black Double Chevron' of Major Erich Gerlitz, *Gruppenkommandeur* III./JG 53, Quotaifiya, July 1942**

Apart from the command insignia and personal rudder tally, the minor differences in finish between this tropical *Friedrich* and that shown immediately above – i.e. the higher dividing line between the tan and blue tones along the fuselage, and the white area of the cowling ring behind the spinner – may be due to this machine's having been taken over from neighbouring JG 27. Erich Gerlitz himself was a recent arrival from II./JG 27 (which he had commanded since December 1941). He would score just two kills while with JG 53 – the last pair of the 18 shown here, in fact – a Kittyhawk west of El Adem on 31 May and a Spitfire near El Alamein on 17 July.

## 23

**Bf 109G-2 'Black 12' of Leutnant Walter Zellot, *Staffelkapitän* 2./JG 53, Tusov/Stalingrad Front, August 1942**

Back briefly to yellow theatre markings, and the first *Gustavs* to wear the 'Ace of Spades' during I. *Gruppe*'s second stint on the Russian front supporting 6. *Armee*'s advance on Stalingrad. Walter Zellot was another whose entire operational career was spent with JG 53. It ended with a score of 85 when he was brought down by Soviet anti-aircraft fire over Vertyaczi, northwest of Stalingrad, on 10 September 1942, exactly one week after having been awarded the Knight's Cross.

## 24

**Bf 109G-4/trop 'Black 1' of Oberleutnant Franz Schiess, *Staffelkapitän* 8./JG 53, Trapani/Sicily, February 1943**

Although pulled out of Tunisia to assist in the aerial defence of Sicily early in December 1942, many 8./JG 53 machines – including the *Kapitän*'s tropicalised *Gustav* 'gunboat' seen here – were still wearing a somewhat tired desert finish over two months later. The 37 kill bars adorning the rudder all refer to victories gained prior to Schiess' assuming command of 8./JG 53 (the last two were for a B-17 and escorting P-38 downed near Bizerta on 29 January 1943 when flying as a member of the *Geschwaderstab*). He would subsequently take his overall score to 67 while leading 8. *Staffel*, before himself falling victim to P-38s off the Gulf of Naples on 2 September 1943.

## 25

**Bf 109G-6/trop 'White 9' of Unteroffizier Georg Amon, 7./JG 53, Sciacca/Sicily, June 1943**

With little flying to do and a lot of spare time on their hands in the first weeks following their return to Sicily in the early summer of 1943, the pilots of 7. *Staffel* had all their new *Gustavs* individually decorated. Each machine featured a cartoon 'Ace of Spades' figure occupying the space between the cockpit and aircraft numeral. Most were engaged in some warlike practice – smashing an English bomber to pieces with a club, shooting a US tank (with a bow and arrow!), snapping an RAF roundel in half, and the like – but Georg Amon, whose nickname was *'Seemann'* ('Sailor'), chose to portray his figure, although clutching a dagger, in more leisurely mode aboard a sailing boat. 'White 9' was lost off Malta on 3 July while being flown by another pilot. 'Sailor' Amon would bail out of a K-4, and into Allied captivity, southwest of Würzburg on 2 April 1945.

## 26

**Bf 109G-6 'Black 2' of Oberfeldwebel Herbert Rollwage, 5./JG 53, Trapani/Sicily, July 1943**

II./JG 53 presumably had no time for such frivolities as individual markings, for Herbert Rollwage's machine presents an altogether more workmanlike appearance from spiralled spinner (a device reportedly introduced to throw bombers' gunners off their aim) to *Schwarmführer's* (section leader's) white rudder with its already imposing scoreboard. The latter, beginning with Rollwage's 11 eastern front kills, currently ends at number 47 – a somewhat mysterious 'Ryan' claimed on 10 July 1943 (but more likely to have been a Vought Kingfisher spotter aircraft from one of the US cruisers bombarding the beachheads on the opening day of the invasion of Sicily).

## 27

**Bf 109G-6 'White 11' of 7./JG 53, Villa Orba/Italy, December 1943**

With a segmented rather than a spiralled spinner (possibly because the pilots of 7. *Staffel*, their days of leisure on Sicily now just a memory, were expected to launch their 21 cm rockets well outside the range of bomber gunners), this 'White 11' may perhaps be the machine in which Leutnant Ernst Höring was lost on 16 January 1944 over northern Italy. His aircraft collided with another *Gustav* during an attack on B-24s.

## 28

**Bf 109G-6 'Black 2' of Unteroffizier Otto Zendler, 8./JG 53, Villa Orba/Italy, December 1944**

Oddly, this 'gunboat' of 8. *Staffel* (note the tightly-spiralled spinner) was also lost in a mid-air collision during the same action of 16 January 1944 as 'White 11' above. But Otto Zendler was reported missing after his machine was hit from above by a crashing P-38 (one of the bombers' escorts) which had just fallen victim to his element leader. Zendler's 'Black 2' and the Lightning both went down together southwest of Klagenfurt, in Austria.

## 29

**Bf 109G-6 'Black 2' of Oberfeldwebel Herbert Rollwage, 5./JG 53, Vienna-Seyring, January 1944**

What a difference six months can make. The appearance of Rollwage's present 'Black 2' (compared to that depicted by profile 26 above) has been changed by the addition of a broad, rust-red fuselage band. This was the colour initially allotted to the ex-*Wilde Sau* Defence of the Reich *Jagdgruppen* (see *Aircraft of the Aces 68 – Bf 109 Defence of the Reich Aces* for further details), and it duly reflects II./JG 53's current 'twinning' with II./JG 301. But note that, during these six months, Rollwage's score has advanced by just two to 49 – the last a brace of P-38s downed on 7 January 1944. All 70+ of Rollwage's victories were scored with JG 53, and it was these that earned him both the Knight's Cross and Oak Leaves (although by the time of the latter award he had been transferred to II./JG 106).

## 30

**Bf 106G-6 'Yellow 1' of Leutnant Alfred Hammer, *Staffelkapitän* 6./JG 53, Vienna-Seyring, February 1944**

Compared to the faded and decidedly greenish-grey hue of Rollwage's 'Black 2' immediately above, Alfred Hammer's obviously brand-new 'gunboat' displays an appreciably darker camouflage finish, albeit enlivened by a similar rust-red band and white rudder, together with yellow numeral and horizontal II. *Gruppe* bar. The last of the 11 victories indicated here was a B-24 downed near Udine, in northeast Italy, on 30 January 1944. This was one of just two 'heavies' among Hammer's final total of 26. He ended the war as the third and final *Kommandeur* of IV./JG 53.

## 31

**Bf 109G-6 'Black 11' of Unteroffizier Heinz Girnth, 8./JG 53, Bad Lippspringe, July 1944**

Yet another brand-new *Gustav*, this aircraft was amongst the batch of G-6s with which III. *Gruppe* was re-equipped after returning from northern Italy to Germany in the summer of 1944. Note the broad spinner spiral and yellow engine cowling, undersides and rudder – but no sign of JG 53's 'official' black Defence of the Reich aft fuselage band. Heinz Girnth would survive the war, latterly as a member of IV. *Gruppe*, with 11 victories.

## 32

**Bf 109G-14/AS 'White 5' of Gefreiter Gerhard Michaelis, 7./JG 53, Hustedt, August 1944**

No sign of a Defence of the Reich band on this late-model *Gustav* either, but this is hardly surprising. It is depicted at Hustedt, in Germany, after II. *Gruppe's* disastrous first foray to the Normandy front on G-6s and during its hurried re-equipment with the G-14/AS variant prior to a second. Upgraded in the interim to four-*Staffel* strength (7./JG 53 was the previous 4./JG 53, and a new 8. *Staffel* had been added), II. *Gruppe's* G-14s fared little better once back in France. Among the casualties was Gerhard Michaelis and his 'White 5', shot down in a dogfight with P-38s on 22 August. Note, after almost five years, the absence of the 'Ace of Spades' badge!

## 33

**Bf 109G-14 'Yellow 9' of 9./JG 53, Neuhausen ob Eck, December 1944**

Also minus the iconic *Geschwader* emblem, this otherwise anonymous tall-tailed, Erla-hooded G-14 of late 1944 may well have been the 'Yellow 9' that three-victory Unteroffizier Hermann Heck was forced to abandon near Pirmasens after III. *Gruppe* ran into P-47s during its abortive New Year's Day 1945 mission against Etain airfield, northwest of Metz, as part of the ill-fated Operation *Bodenplatte*.

## 34

**Bf 109K-4 'Yellow 1' of Leutnant Günther Landt, *Staffelkapitän* 11./JG 53, Kirrlach, February 1945**
Although the unit badge has disappeared for good from JG 53's western-based *Gruppen*, this K-4 in typical late-war green/brown finish does at least sport the *Geschwader*'s black aft fuselage band. Note, however, that early in 1945, for some unknown reason, the yellow that had previously served to identify 9. *Staffel* machines (see immediately above) was transferred to 11. *Staffel*, with 9./JG 53 now using white numerals. Günther Landt remained at the head of 11./JG 53 until war's end, by which time his score stood at 23.

## 35

**Bf 109G-14/AS 'White 8' of 7./JG 53, Malmsheim, March 1945**
This 7. *Staffel* machine poses an even greater puzzle – why is it wearing neither a fuselage cross nor a tailfin swastika? Conditions were admittedly chaotic in the closing weeks of the war, but this can hardly have been an oversight. Has 'White 9' been repainted and the national insignia not yet re-applied? Or is this perhaps a personal statement on the part of the unknown pilot along the lines of the infamous 'red band' affair at the time of the Battle of Britain – and, if so, why retain the underwing crosses? Just another of the myriad minor mysteries that still surround the wartime Luftwaffe.

## UNIT HERALDRY

### 1

JG 53
worn on cowling of Bf 109E/F/G

### 2

10.(N)/JG 72
worn beneath windscreen of Ar 68E/F

### 3

10.(*Jabo*)/JG 53
worn on aft fuselage of Bf 109F

## BIBLIOGRAPHY

**BEALE, NICK, et al.,** *Air War Italy 1944-45*. Airlife, Shrewsbury, 1996

**CONSTABLE, TREVOR J and TOLIVER, COL RAYMOND F,** *Horrido! Fighter Aces of the Luftwaffe*. Macmillan, New York, 1968

**FOREEL, MAJ FRITZ von,** *Mölders und seine Männer*. Steirische Verlagsanstalt, Graz, 1941

**FRAPPE, JEAN-BERNARD,** *La Luftwaffe face au débarquement allié, 6 Juin au 30 août 1944*. Editions Heimdal, Bayeux, 1999

**FREEMAN, ROGER A,** *Mighty Eighth War Diary*. Jane's, London, 1976

**GIRBIG, WERNER,** *Start im Morgengrauen*. Motorbuch Verlag, Stuttgart, 1973

**HAMMEL, ERIC,** *Air War Europe*. Pacifica Press, California, 1994

**HELD, WERNER,** *Reichsverteidigung: Die Deutsche Tagjagd 1943-1945*. Podzun-Pallas, Friedberg, 1998

**KUROWSKI, FRANZ,** *Balkenkreuz und Roter Stern*. Podzun-Pallas, Friedberg, 1986

**LIPFERT, HELMUT,** *Das Tagebuch des Hauptmann Lipfert*. Motorbuch Verlag, Stuttgart, 1973

**MEIMBERG, JULIUS,** *Feindberührung: Erinnerungen 1939-1945*. NeunundzwanzigSechs Verlag, Moosburg, 2002

**MEINERT, KURT und TEUBER, REINHARD,** *Die deutsche Luftwaffe 1939-1945*. Militär-Verlag Patzwall, Norderstedt, 1996

**NOWARRA, HEINZ J,** *Luftwaffen-Einsatz 'Barbarossa' 1941*. Podzun-Pallas Verlag, Friedberg, undated

**OBERMAIER, ERNST,** *Die Ritterkreuzträger der Luftwaffe: Band 1, Jagdflieger*. Verlag Dieter Hoffmann, Mainz 1966

**PRIEN, JOCHEN, et al.,** *Chronik des JG 53 'Pik-As' (3 vols)*. Flugzeug Dokumentation/struve-druck, Eutin, 1989-1991

**PRIEN, JOCHEN,** *Die Jagdverbände der Deutschen Luftwaffe 1934 bis 1945 (various vols)*. struve-druck, Eutin, from 2000

**RUST, KENN C,** *Fifteenth Air Force Story*. Historical Aviation Album, Temple City, 1976

**SHORES, CHRISTOPHER & RING, HANS,** *Fighters over the Desert*. Neville Spearman, London, 1969

**SHORES, CHRISTOPHER, et al.,** *Fighters over Tunisia*. Neville Spearman, London, 1975

**SHORES, CHRISTOPHER, et al.,** *Malta - The Hurricane Years 1940-41*. Grub Street, London, 1987

**SHORES, CHRISTOPHER, et al.,** *Malta - The Spitfire Year 1942*. Grub Street, London, 1991

**SHORES, CHRISTOPHER, et al.,** *Fledgling Eagles*. Grub Street, London, 1991

**ZENTNER, CHRISTIAN,** *Lexikon des Zweiten Weltkriegs*. Südwest Verlag, Munich, 1977

# INDEX

References to illustrations are shown in **bold**. Plates are shown with page and caption locators in brackets.